Chakras for Beginners

Discover How to Balance the Chakras with Secret Healing Techniques

Barbara Nara

HEALING TECHNIQUES PRESS

CONTENTS

Chapter 1 - Introducing the Chakras

Let us begin by introducing you to the idea of a chakra. The word chakra comes from Sanskrit, and it can be taken to mean the energy wheel. Energy is all around us, vibrating at different frequencies. Indeed, energy fills the entire universe, even in dimensions that we cannot normally perceive (these are the spiritual realms). The universe is full of life force energy that fills the entirety of all that there is or has ever been. It flows through the body, and we interact with it daily.

What Are Chakras?

A chakra is a point in the body where energy gathers on its journey to flow through the body so that we can function at optimal, healthy levels. There are seven major chakras in the body, and many more minor chakras. In this book, our focus will be on the major chakras because this has the most significant impact on healing and well-being.

Chakras can become blocked, and when this happens, there is not a proper flow and distribution of energy throughout the body. This can lead to illnesses and ill health of various kinds. Furthermore, the unhealthy state that takes place when proper energy flows are not realized can result in problems in the physical body, the mental/emotional body, and the spiritual body. Therefore, healing the chakras can have an impact on every aspect of your health.

Chakras can also be out of balance. As we will see, the chakras provide energy for different aspects of our being, and when they are out of balance, certain parts of ourselves can become overactive, leading to dysfunctional behaviors or ill health.

Each chakra vibrates at a different energetic frequency. Light also does the same. As such, the chakras are all associated with different colors, ranging from lower energy to higher energy. The energetic vibrational colors going from lower energy to the highest energy are red, orange, yellow, green, blue, indigo, and purple. It is no coincidence that these are also the colors of the rainbow.

A chakra is also associated with an element and a location in the body. The chakras are not energy themselves, but locations where energy congregates. In a healthy individual, that energy flows freely and unimpeded, interacting with the body, mind, and soul, as well as the universe beyond leading to a healthy balance. When all of your chakras are open and balanced completely, you will feel a sense of harmony, peace, and contentment.

The root chakra is the most fundamental of the chakras. It "roots" you to Mother Earth, providing you with fundamental grounding. It is associated with safety, security, and being able to provide for your basic needs, such as food, water, and shelter. The **feeling** of being safe and secure is closely associated with the root chakra. The location of the root chakra is at the base of the spine, and the associated color is red. This reflects the fact that the vibrational frequency of the root chakra is the lowest of the seven major chakras.

Sacral Chakra

Just above the root chakra, we have the sacral chakra. It is associated with sexuality, the ability to feel pleasure, and your creativity. It has a higher vibrational frequency than the root chakra because it involves higher functions of your being. Most people are not going to be feeling pleasure and creativity if they have not met the most fundamental needs of their security, like being able to procure food and water. The sacral chakra is located just below the navel.

Solar Plexus Chakra

The solar plexus chakra is associated with higher-level functioning of the ego. This includes self-confidence, a sense of purpose in your career, and taking responsibility. When you have a balanced and open root, sacral, and solar plexus chakras, you are able to take responsibility for your life and act with confidence and self-discipline. The color associated with the solar plexus chakra is yellow. It is located just above the navel and below the rib cage.

Heart Chakra

The heart chakra is associated with love, empathy, tolerance, and acceptance. This is not just romantic love, although romantic love is definitely associated with the heart chakra. All types of love, including self-love and self-acceptance, come from the heart chakra. The color of the heart chakra is green, although pink colored stones and crystals also work well when healing the heart chakra. The heart chakra is located in the center of the chest.

Throat Chakra

The throat chakra is the first spiritual chakra, located in the lower throat area. As you might guess from the location, the throat chakra is involved with communication and speaking the truth. The color of the throat chakra is blue.

Third Eye Chakra

The third eye chakra is located in the brow region at the center, and above the physical eyes. It is also associated with a small organ in the brain called the pineal gland. The third eye has been long known since ancient times to be our eye into the realms of intuition and the psychic world. Therefore, this is an "eye" that gets information from non-physical planes of existence. We all have intuitive abilities, but if the third eye is blocked, we cannot access them. Fortunately, it is possible to heal and open your third eye chakra. This is a very energetic chakra. The color associated with the third eye chakra is indigo.

Crown Chakra

The crown chakra is located at the top of the head, or according to some experts, it is slightly above the top of the head. It is closely associated with the brain and the nervous system. As its most basic function, the crown chakra is associated with consciousness and awareness. However, it goes well beyond this because the crown chakra connects us with our spirituality and Higher Self. It is associated with wisdom, presence, and bliss. At the most fundamental level, the crown chakra is associated with communion with higher states of being and the spiritual oneness of the universe. The main color of the crown chakra is purple, but it is also associated with white and gold.

How Are Chakras Healed?

In the following pages, we will be discussing symptoms that a chakra is blocked or out of balance. If you determine that are you are suffering from blocked chakras, you are not alone. In western society, especially in the modern world, most people are living unhealthy and unbalanced lives. It would be a fair wager to guess that most people are out of balance when it comes to their chakras. Unfortunately, because of our increasingly materialistic and atheistic beliefs, many people are not even aware of this or willing to consider the prospect that they need more than physical healing.

There are many ways that you can heal, balance, and awaken your chakras. The primary method that is used is daily meditation. We will discuss ways that you can meditate a few minutes a day that will go a long way toward healing the chakras.

Chakras can also be healed using yoga, daily affirmations, and by the proper use of colors. Many people also use crystals because of their vibrational characteristics and ability to store and transmit vibrational spiritual energy. The vibrational frequencies that are associated with the chakras are related to the spiritual components or essence associated with the meaning of each of the chakras.

In the following sections, we will introduce the seven major chakras. Each will be explored in more detail, with a chapter devoted to each in the book.

Balancing the Chakras

In the chapters that follow, we are going to go into detail on the symptoms that a given chakra is blocked, as well as the specific procedures for healing and unblocking each of the seven major chakras. Here, we will outline the general procedures that are used to heal your chakras.

If you are a beginner, there is going to be a temptation to rush right to the spiritual chakras. However, chances are, if you are new to this way of thinking, that you have at least some level of blockages occurring in your lower chakras. It is essential, for the purposes of maintaining the correct balance, that you heal the lower chakras before you attempt to work with the higher-level chakras. For example, imagine that you have a blocked root chakra, and you are having problems maintaining the basics of your life. You are going to be filled with many negative energies that are going to impact and block your higher-level chakras as well. If you are feeling unsafe and anxious all the time because of the blocked root chakra, are you going to be able to devote energy to unconditional love, speaking the truth, and your psychic abilities? Maybe some people can manage to do so, but the reality is the vast majority of people will not be able to pull this off. Look at this like building a house. You build the foundation first, and if the foundation is not constructed correctly, the rest of the house is unstable and unsafe. You are on a lifelong spiritual journey, so be patient as you pursue your goals. There will be greater rewards for those who are patient.

There are seven ways that you can heal and balance your chakras to promote maximum physical, mental, emotional, and spiritual health. We briefly describe each of these below.

Meditation

Meditation helps on many levels. The process of meditation will free the mind and calm your nerves. During meditation, you can use visualization techniques to work with each of the chakras. We will be discussing the details and basic meditation methods in the following chapters.

Yoga

While it's not required that you do yoga, it can be a great tool for those who do so. Yoga will help you to physically open up your chakras to promote natural energy flow. It also has many benefits for the body, promoting both flexibility and toning, in addition to helping you heal and balance your chakras.

Breathing

Deep breathing exercises can be done independently or in conjunction with meditation and yoga. Deep breathing helps to calm the nerves and open up the flow of energy in the body.

Vocalization and Sound

There are many ways to associate a sound with healing the chakras. For example, you can use single tones or mantras. You can also say daily affirmations that will help to "reprogram" your subconscious mind and help you to reach your goals. Music can also help assist you in your efforts.

Colors

Each of the seven major chakras is associated with a given color that reflects the vibrational energy level. When you are working on a given chakra, you can surround yourself with the colors associated with it. This can be done with clothing and crystals that you wear, carry with you, or use in your meditation. It also includes colors that are used to fill the home and a location you use for meditation and/or yoga exercises.

Food

Choosing the right foods that you need to heal your chakras is also important. Here, you can use color as your guide. Westerners are not used to thinking in these terms, but the coloration of a given food item is associated with its energy level. As an example, if you are working on healing the root chakra, you would want to increase the number and variety of red-colored foods in your diet.

Essential Oils

Another way to help you heal your chakras is to use essential oils. Each essential oil is also vibrating at a specific energetic frequency. You can apply essential oils to the skin or breathe in the smells.

In the next chapter, we will start at the lowest chakra, the root chakra. We will explore the root chakra in detail, discussing the symptoms of blockage so that readers can determine whether or not their root chakra is blocked.

Chapter 2 - History of the Chakras

The chakras, as a concept of energy centers of the body, entered into the western mindset more than 100 years ago. However, the origin of these concepts actually goes much further than that. The chakras originated in Tantrik traditions as energy centers. In that view, during ancient times, they were not considered to be origins of energy but rather to be focal points where energy congregated on its way to flow throughout the body.

Originally, these energy centers were not taken to be physical realities but were empirically based. That is, they were based on observation. It was noted where human beings experienced various emotions and sensations, connecting the physical to the mental, emotional, and spiritual states, which we all experience.

So in a sense, these were symbolic, conceptual ideas, and yet they were related to actual, empirical, and physical observations. Later, over the period of 1500 to 500 BC, these ideas became further elevated and developed, where they were written down in ancient Indian texts called the Vedas. This is where they became associated with the concept of spinning wheels of energy and light. These concepts were studied and developed for more than a thousand years and were codified in more modern form in the 1600s in the writings of a famous Indian guru named Swami Purandanda. Toward the start of the 20TH century, the ideas of Swami Purandanda were translated into English, where they gradually gained popularity and acceptance in different parts of the western world. Knowledge of the chakras and the practice of yoga became widespread after the 1960s.

Chapter 3 - The Root Chakra

The root chakra is the lowest and most fundamental of the seven major chakras. It is located at the base of the spine. The color of the root chakra is red, and it is symbolically represented using four lotus leaves. The Sanskrit name of the root chakra is **Muladhara**.

What Is the Root Chakra?

The root chakra is located at the base of the spine and extends up the lowest three vertebrae. The main function of the root chakra is to give you your sense of safety and security. Anhara is a Sanskrit word that means **support**.

Therefore, you can literally translate the word Muladhara as "root support."

The root chakra is considered to be a **matter** chakra. What this means is that this chakra is associated with your physical well-being. The root chakra means you have your feet firmly planted on the earth, and you are safe and secure, which, in turn, means that you are able to meet all of your basic needs. The most basic needs that every one of us must meet include safety, food, water, and shelter.

Due to the importance of money in satisfying these needs in the modern world, the root chakra is also associated with basic financial security. This does not mean that it is associated with getting wealthy or even earning a good income. The root chakra is only associated with earning enough money to satisfy your basic needs, as well as being financially stable.

The root chakra can be likened to the foundation of a house. If you are building a house that you plan to live in for the next twenty or thirty years, you are not going to rush the construction and ignore the foundation or rush it. A solid foundation must be laid in order to build a good, solid, and safe house. This is how you promote stability for your life.

The needs expressed in or associated with the root chakra must be satisfied in order to fully open any of the higher chakras. When we list the symptoms of having a root chakra that is blocked, you may feel that your root chakra is healthy. Nonetheless, I advise anyone who is new to the study of chakras, meditation, and yoga to work on the root chakra to ensure that it is healthy and fully opened. If you are a beginner, it is highly likely that your chakras are not properly open and balanced.

So please be patient and take your time working through the chakras. Learning to do it properly will help you in the years to come.

The root chakra is also associated with many basic emotions, some of which are unhealthy. If you are suffering from anxiety, fear, and doubt, this may be because your root chakra is blocked. Trust is also something that can be closely associated with the root chakra (and of course, trust can be associated with other chakras, as well). An inability to trust other people is often rooted in fear. Anxiety can also be caused by a general sense of fear, being unsafe, and not being in control of your life.

Having the sense that you are basically in control of your life is a part of having a balanced root chakra.

How the Root Chakra Gets Blocked

The root chakra can be blocked by many experiences, but life during your childhood has a large impact on the root chakra. When you are a small child, you are very tuned into the feeling of safety. If you had loving parents who were stable and who provided a stable home life, then as a child, you felt completely safe. This is likely to carry over to adulthood, but of course, there can be events throughout your life that can disrupt the root chakra.

One of the ways that the root chakra can become blocked is that during childhood, a child may experience erratic care. Having their needs met only on a sporadic and unpredictable basis, the child will soon have a blocked root chakra. Any abuse during childhood will certainly lead to a blockage of the root chakra. Inconsistent treatment during childhood can also block the root chakra. A moody caregiver can have a negative impact, as the child never knows when the parent is going to be angry, leading to feelings of fear and insecurity.

Any negative experience that significantly impacts your ability to feel safe, or to trust other individuals, can also block the root chakra. Sexual assault and rape are major reasons that many people, especially women, have a blocked root chakra. This is one way that a root chakra can become blocked in adulthood. Another event that can lead to a blocked chakra at any time is a break-in in the home. This leaves people feeling unsafe and violated, even if they were not at home during the break-in.

Symptoms of a Blocked Root Chakra

Many symptoms of a blocked root chakra are related to a generalized feeling of anxiety. If you feel unsafe, this is definitely a sign of a blockage in their root chakra. This feeling of being unsafe can take many forms. If you feel unsafe while at home, this is a definite sign of a root chakra that is blocked. Many people feel unsafe at home and want to move to a better location, but they are unable to do so because of financial reasons. This is a definite symptom of a blocked root chakra because you have the feeling of unsafety coupled with an inability to meet your financial needs.

Financial insecurity is an indicator of a root chakra that is blocked. This can take the form of never having enough money to pay all of your bills or amassing large amounts of debt that interfere with satisfying your basic needs. It can also take the form of instability, such as irregular income or other problems. If you have any problems managing your finances, you should suspect a blocked root chakra.

Anxiety disorders, a constant feeling of fear and uncertainty, and nightmares are common symptoms of having a blockage in the root chakra. These may or may not be coupled with a feeling of restlessness. If you lack a foundational grounding in your life, then you are naturally going to feel restless. This is coupled with a general sense of insecurity because you will have a sense (consciously or not) that you are unable to meet your basic needs.

Since many people get a blocked root chakra due to inconsistent treatment or actual abandonment during childhood, they may have a vague sense of feeling abandoned as adults. If you are feeling abandoned, this is a strong indication that you should work on healing your root chakra.

The inability to meet your financial needs can lead to other problems, such as co-dependency. You may be relying on friends, family, or other relatives to constantly bail you out of your latest financial problem or just lend you cash on a regular basis to make ends meet. When thinking about this, borrowing $50 from people here and there is not necessarily a symptom. But if you regularly have to borrow money from people to get by, then this indicates a blocked root chakra.

Having to depend on others to meet your basic needs, or simply not being able to securely meet them, can lead to feelings of guilt and resentment. Depression can also result from these situations, and you may also experience feelings of helplessness.

A blockage of a chakra impacts all aspects of your being. If you have a blocked root chakra, it is so fundamental that you may not be able to experience anything related to the other chakras. You are going to lack self-confidence and become unable to truly experience sexuality and pleasure or express your creativity. In this case, spirituality may be completely out of reach.

In addition, there are going to be physical symptoms in many people. The physical symptoms associated with the root chakra usually impact the lower parts of the body. Sciatica is common, and you may feel chronic foot and leg pain. You can have digestive issues, including diarrhea and constipation, on a regular basis. Prostate problems in men, urinary tract infections, and menstruation problems in women can also be symptoms.

Foods to Heal the Root Chakra

As a part of healing the root chakra, you can spend some time eating foods that are specifically helpful for this purpose. Begin by considering root vegetables. As they grow in the earth, they contain foundational energy vibrations that can help heal your root chakra. These include potatoes, carrots, radishes, onions, and garlic. You can also focus on consuming foods that have a red color. Tomatoes are an excellent food to consume while working on your root chakra. Beets are an excellent choice because they have a reddish color, in addition to being a root vegetable. Sweet potatoes and pumpkin seeds can also be helpful.

Essential Oils for the Root Chakra

When using essential oils to help you heal the root chakra, consider using oils that are calming. A good example of essential oils for the root chakra is sandalwood. This essential oil can help you to calm the nervous system, which will help to release the negative energies that are associated with the anxiety and feelings of fear. Myrrh is also a good essential oil that can be utilized when working with the root chakra. It also has a gentle, calming effect on the nervous system.

Colors for the Root Chakra

You can use colors to help heal the root chakra. The main color to use when healing the root chakra is red. In order to use colors, there are many things that you can do during your healing period. The first thing is to wear red-colored items of clothing. This can be done at any time, but a special situation to consider is when you either do yoga or engage in meditation. You can also fill your home with red-colored items. This can include pillows, sheets, throws, and drapes. The goal is to constantly surround yourself with the energy of the root chakra. This energy vibration is strongly associated with the red color.

You can also place red flowers throughout your home or in your office. Paintings that have a lot of red in them can also be hung on the walls. If you are in need of healing of the root chakra, surrounding yourself with as much of this red energy as possible can be very beneficial.

Crystals for the Root Chakra

Crystals can play a central role in healing your chakras. For details, please see my book on **Crystal Healing**. For the root chakra, the crystals that you want to use are those that are red or black in color. The energy of the crystal, more so than the specific color, is important for its function. Four crystals that are strongly recommended include garnet, hematite, black tourmaline, and obsidian. Ruby is also an excellent choice. If you feel unsafe in your living space, consider using four stones of black tourmaline, and place one in each corner of the room. You can also place crystals in your car, or wear them to help heal the root chakra, reduce your anxiety, and increase your sense of safety.

Try holding hematite in your hands, either just for calming or during meditation. It is said that simply holding this crystal can help you feel centered and secure.

Meditation for the Root Chakra

Meditation is going to be the most important tool for healing the chakras. There are some variations on mediation that can be used, but in this book for beginners, we are going to focus on the most standard method of meditation. This involves the visualization of a spinning wheel of energy that has the appropriate color for the given chakra that we are working with.

Before you begin meditation, the first thing to consider is where you are going to meditate, when, and how long. You can meditate once or twice per day. At a minimum, you should meditate for 15 minutes per session. If you have the time, meditating for 30 minutes is acceptable, as well.

Don't worry if you have trouble meditating in the beginning. If you are new to meditation, it may take time to train your mind to focus. Being able to focus and rid the mind of thought is one of the important aspects of meditation. People have active minds, you are probably always wondering about something, having conversations with yourself, or maybe your mind is filled with worry. Certainly, if you have a blocked root chakra, you are going to have an overactive mind filled with worry, thinking about how you are going to pay your bills or wishing you could move or other issues. When meditating, your aim is to completely calm the mind, so you shouldn't have any inner voices or ideas flowing through your head.

The space where you meditate should be comfortable and quiet, and if you live with others or have children in the house, you need to ensure that you are going to be able to meditate without being disturbed. You can include soft Indian, Chinese, or Japanese music in the room if desired, or you can meditate in silence.

The position used for meditation is called the easy pose, which is called **Sukhasana** in Sanskrit. This is basically sitting on the floor with your legs crossed in front of you. If you feel uncomfortable, you can sit on a pillow. When you are beginning, you can also sit against a wall or other object to give yourself some back support.

To begin the meditation process, close your eyes, and breathe slowly and deeply. Spend a few minutes concentrating on your breath, clearing your mind of any thoughts. To help yourself clear your mind, focus on the breath. Breathe naturally, or if it makes you feel more relaxed, you can breathe in through your nose and then exhale through the mouth.

Now, begin to visualize a completely black space. It

should be the darkest black you can imagine, an inky dark blackness. Now see a distant red light. Slowly imagine this red light, which can be either a slowly spinning disk or a spinning lotus flower with four petals, as shown in the illustration at the beginning of this chapter.

See it slowly getting larger and larger as it comes closer to you. Now, imagine it entering your body, slowly rising up to the location at the base of your spine where the root chakra is. As it gets closer, see it get larger and larger. When you visualize it entering your root chakra, see it spinning faster. Now, when you inhale, see the disk of light or flower grow in size, and then see it shrink when you exhale. Keep up this exercise until you have reached your time limit for meditating.

You can also say the LAM mantra while meditating to help set the right energy level.

Affirmations for the Root Chakra

Affirmations are statements that we can say to ourselves in order to help train our subconscious mind. A lot of the blockage in a chakra can be due to beliefs that are held in the subconscious. They were programmed in there by caregivers and experiences that may have been with us long ago. As a result, you may not even be fully aware of the belief systems that are governing your life. Saying affirmations every day can help to reverse these thought patterns.

Here are some examples that can be used to help heal the root chakra:

- I am safe.

- I am protected.

- I am able to take care of my needs.

30

- Mother Earth will care for me and protect me.

- I am safe at home.

- I feel safe and secure.

You can say these affirmations and hold a crystal in your hand to help enhance the energy. Say the affirmations as often as needed, but at least once a day. Saying them prior to going to bed is a good way to ensure that they enter into the subconscious mind.

Chapter 4 - The Sacral Chakra

In this chapter, we come to the second chakra, which is the sacral chakra. The sacral chakra is going to have a chance to flourish if the root chakra is healed and opened. As we will see, it is important to have a balance with the chakras. Too much of one chakra at the expense of other chakras can create a lot of problems in your life, just as blockages will do so. Therefore, it is important to make sure that you are healing your chakras, but you also want to make sure that you are not paying excessive attention to one chakra.

The color of the sacral chakra is orange, and it is represented using six lotus petals. In Sanskrit, the name of the Sacral Chakra is **Svadhishthana**. The sacral chakra, like the root chakra, is a matter chakra.

What Is the Sacral Chakra?

The sacral chakra is associated with sexuality, the ability to experience pleasure, and creativity. It is also associated with reproductive functions and raw emotions. Due to its association with sexuality and reproduction, the sacral chakra is important in relationships, sensuality, and the feelings associated with them. Fantasies, including sexual fantasies but also any fantasy of any kind due to the association of this chakra with the creative juices of the human spirit, are also associated with an open and balanced sacral chakra.

The sacral chakra is one chakra where balance is important. You can see this in simple observations of how people live their lives and the problems that they may have. If the sacral chakra is open but unbalanced, this can lead to addictive behaviors. Many people suffer from sexual addiction. When this happens, they will devote far too much energy and attention in pursuing sexual partners and engaging in sexual activity. This can lead to destructive results as other aspects of their lives suffer because they are not in proper balance. The key to the sacral chakra is being able to enjoy pleasures of all kinds, without being overwhelmed by it.

Since the sacral chakra is not only associated with sexuality but also with sensuality and experiencing pleasure of all kinds, an out-of-balance sacral chakra can manifest in many different ways. Many people with this type of unbalance will become gambling addicts. When the sacral and root chakras are out of balance, this can lead to disastrous results. Not only will they be devoting excessive attention to gambling, becoming literally obsessed, but they will also have money management problems, as well. They routinely find themselves broke and desperately seeking out money (hoping to devote most of it toward more gambling).

Another interesting way that an out-of-balance sacral chakra can manifest is that a person may devote too much energy to fantasies. It is normal to fantasize to a certain degree. This can include imagining sexual fantasies in your mind or seeing yourself living in a different place or time, or playing a different role in life as compared to physical reality. However, when these fantasies become dominant and start interfering with your actual life, fantasies are destructive. Using sexual fantasies as an example, some people become so overwhelmed by sexual fantasies that they block out real sexual relationships with other people. Or they might have nonsexual fantasies that can be described as big dreams that never materialize. In this case, people may imagine themselves as having stronger possibilities than are realistically possible. Of course, it is healthy to dream big, provided you take practical steps to achieve your goals. The key to understanding a big dreamer who has an out-of-balance sacral chakra is the fact that they are always dreaming of doing different things, but they never actually take any steps to implement any of them. It is one thing to take steps toward a goal and fail; it's another thing to have big thoughts and be a big talker, without taking any steps to achieve anything.

Drug and alcohol addiction will also be due to an out-of-balance sacral chakra, in whole or in part. Sometimes, addictions happen because the sacral chakra is blocked, and people are unable to truly experience a pleasure. When this occurs, they find themselves constantly seeking out pleasure but are never able to really attain it, or they have a very high threshold for experiencing even the remotest sensations of it. This leads them to seek out a risk-taking lifestyle, with sexual behavior, substance abuse, and other addictions. Extreme athletes are also often suffering from a blocked sacral chakra, having to take on riskier and riskier activities to attain even the faintest hints of enjoyment.

As you learn about the other chakras, you will also be able to see how problems in one chakra may be related to difficulties in the other chakras. These types of problems often don't occur in isolation because people who have blocked chakras are generally unhealthy when considering the whole being and soul of the individual. After all, if you were on a solid spiritual path, studying the chakras, prana, and kundalini energy, and regularly practicing yoga and meditation, your problems would be minimized.

For this reason, during the study of the chakras, it is a good exercise to look at each chakra and think about how they can interrelate when it comes to the actual feelings and behavior that is expressed in the overall direction of your life. We already gave an example with a person with a gambling problem because of sacral chakra issues and how they may have financial issues because of root chakra problems as well. In sexual relationships, problems with the sacral chakra can cause problems with the heart chakra and vice versa.

Another example is anxiety that can result from root chakra blockages. When there are high levels of anxiety, this can manifest in many different behaviors that are destructive. For example, some people seek to alleviate their anxiety with pleasure-seeking. This can include any number of things we have already talked about, but sexual activity and substance abuse are often the go-to addictions that can result from attempts to alleviate anxiety.

Alternatively, if you don't feel secure and grounded because you are having problems with your root chakra, you might develop a lot of anxiety that inhibits your ability to engage in sexual relationships. You might become withdrawn and prone to fantasy. The two chakras can be blocked simultaneously, or problems in your root chakra might even lead to a blockage in the sacral chakra.

So, what does a healthy sacral chakra look like? When you have a sacral chakra, you are easily able to experience the many pleasures that life has to offer. You are able to experience sexuality and sexual pleasures, and you can enjoy them to the fullest. This is without becoming overwhelmed or interfering with other aspects of your life. You are able to fill your life with pleasures like drinking alcohol, enjoying good meals, and enjoying sensuality. The basic emotions of the lower centers of the body can be experienced with raw intensity but kept in perspective. Yet your life will be balanced completely, and your enjoyment of pleasure will not interfere with your work life or lead to the development of destructive relationships filled with jealousy, multiple partners, and constant drama.

The element that is most closely associated with the sacral chakra is water. It is symbolic of the flow that comes with healthy pleasure and sensuality. Every one of the senses is alive and experienced intensely when your sacral chakra is open and healthy, so you are able to enjoy smell, taste, touch, sight, and sound. The association with water also reflects the fact that a healthy sacral chakra is associated with flexibility. Physically, the sacral chakra is also associated with the free flow of the lymphatic system and blood and the circulatory system. This also includes the free flow of reproductive fluids.

The flowing nature of the sacral chakra is not only literal in terms of movement of fluids in the body, but it is also symbolic of the free flow of creative thoughts and fantasies. If your sacral chakra is healthy, creative thoughts and ideas **flow** naturally through your mind. You will experience creativity without effort, and it will seem completely normal and natural.

Another way that the flowing nature of the sacral chakra will manifest is flexibility in relationships with other people. If you have a blocked sacral chakra, your relationships with other people (especially sexual relationships) will be characterized by difficulty, as if you are constantly running into a **wall** or resistance (blocking the flow). Sexual relationships may come to dominate your time and energy, even outside the sexuality itself or any sexual addictions. In contrast, when the sacral chakra is open and healthy, you will find your relationships come effortlessly and function smoothly, and you are able to come and go from it with ease.

By enhancing the ability to feel all five physical senses to the fullest, opening the sacral chakra will help you feel and experience the physical and material world. The enjoyment of the senses will lead you to enjoy and experience the pleasures of food, fine clothing and goods, beautiful cars, and other fine things in life but without being overwhelmed by it. In other words, the experience of luxury is another aspect of the sacral chakra.

To summarize, the sacral chakra is associated with sexuality, the experience of pleasure and sensuality, basic low-level emotions, and creativity.

How the Sacral Chakra Gets Blocked?

There are many ways that the sacral chakra can become blocked. Any type of sexual abuse, rape, or assault is an obvious cause of a sacral chakra blockage. If this is the cause of a blockage, a long and intense process of working on the sacral chakra is going to be necessary.

A blockage of the sacral chakra can also happen when an early relationship goes sour in dramatic fashion. If it is a person's first sexual relationship, and there are issues of betrayal or other emotional abuses, this can lead to a blockage of the sacral chakra.

Many other things can lead to a blockage of the sacral chakra. For example, if parents have strange aversions to a healthy view of sexuality, they can cause the sacral chakra to become blocked in childhood. Often, this is something that is passed down from generation to generation, and puritan views of sexuality have, in many cases, led to a cultural-wide phenomenon with problems related to the sacral chakra. Even now, although sexuality is more open and accepted in western cultures, puritan heritage is still influential. The puritan view of life also goes beyond the expression of sexuality. It also discourages the enjoyment of pleasure generally. We are often not conscious of how the puritan view is influencing us, but it is still a large factor in American culture, leading people to **feel** that pleasure is "dirty." When something is felt rather than believed logically, it has far more power, and it gets ingrained in the subconscious mind, and a blockage of the sacral chakra can happen.

The explosion of pornography is an important thing to consider and a difficult thing for people to talk about. With free pornography available all over the internet, people are getting the sacral chakra blocked. This does not mean that people should not look at pornography, but it is very easy to do so and then end up with a blocked or unbalanced sacral chakra. The first danger that comes out of it is that it can lead to an obsession with sexuality. Second, it can drive a person to become too prone to fantasy. When you are living in a fantasy life, this can prevent you from having real sexual relationships, and you might develop "high standards" that are unrealistic as a result of spending too much time fantasizing with pornography.

Pornography, paradoxically, can dull the sacral chakra. After too much pornography, a person may actually lose interest in sexuality or pleasure-seeking. Nothing seems to satisfy. Care must be taken if you are going to expose yourself to this material.

Symptoms of a Sacral Chakra Blockage

As we noted in the previous two sections, a blockage of the sacral chakra can often manifest in opposite ways. The first way that a blocked sacral chakra can manifest is that you become dull to the world. You will feel uninspired and unable to experience pleasure. You may find that your sexual desires drop off by a large amount, and you might not have any sexual desires at all.

This emotional dullness can expand into any area where sensual pleasure is a component of life. If the sacral chakra blockage is severe, you might find yourself unable to enjoy eating and drinking. Food may become boring and tasteless, and although you may eat because you are driven to do so by survival, you won't enjoy eating or have much of an appetite.

A sacral chakra blockage can have an impact on the root chakra as well, so feelings of fear and anxiety may result from this blockage. You might find yourself avoiding sexual relationships with other people. Sometimes, low self-esteem, when it comes to your view of your own sexual attractiveness, may be the result. You might also engage in overeating as a "self-fulfilling prophecy," where your subconscious is working to make you less sexually attractive.

A low sense of self-worth can lead people with a blocked sacral chakra toward unhealthy and abusive relationships if they are involved in relationships at all. Fear and jealousy will characterize these relationships, arising from the insecurity and low self-esteem that come from a blocked sacral chakra. Depression is common when there is a long-term blockage of the sacral chakra.

Physical symptoms that are related to sexuality and reproduction are a natural extension of a sacral chakra blockage. Often, they serve to function as excuses to avoid sexual relationships. Urinary tract infections will be frequent. Impotence is common in men with a blocked sacral chakra, along with other performance issues. Women may have vaginal dryness or other problems such as menstruation problems, and both sexes may have infertility issues.

Other physical symptoms of a blocked sacral chakra include bladder and kidney stones, gynecological cysts, constipation, and back pain.

If you have a blocked sacral chakra, you might find yourself devoting too much time and energy to fantasy. This can include fantasies of a sexual nature, often accompanied by excessive masturbation. This may interfere with your ability to establish and enjoy sexual relationships with other people. Beyond sexual fantasies, people with a blocked sexual chakra may find themselves so engaged in a fantasy that their real-life their creativity is lost.

As we discussed earlier, you have to be on alert for an out-of-balance sacral chakra, as well. The symptoms of this are basically too much energy devoted to pleasure-seeking and addictive behaviors. You are out of balance in your life if you engage in these activities, for example, drinking alcohol every single night to the point of intoxication, devoting all of your free time and money to gambling, being obsessed with food and eating, or being sexually obsessed. These are symptoms that you need to work on and bring the sacral chakra into balance.

Foods for the Sacral Chakra

Eating the right foods can help balance and heal the sacral chakra. Fortunately, the natural world is full of foods that can assist you when working with the sacral chakra. Also, these foods are often beneficial for the root chakra, so you can heal and balance both simultaneously. Not to mention that many of these foods are extremely healthy. Keep the color orange in mind when seeking out foods for this purpose.

Foods that can help both the root and sacral chakra include carrots and sweet potatoes. This is because they have deep orange colors, while also being root vegetables that promote grounding and security.

Other foods that help balance the sacral chakra include oranges, orange juice, orange peppers, mangos, orange cantaloupe, peaches, and apricots. Salmon is an excellent protein source that can help with both the root and sacral chakra. Eating beef steak can also help to heighten sexual energy. Almonds and walnuts are also reported to help heal the sacral chakra. Since the element of the sacral chakra is water, drinking adequate amounts of pure water to stay hydrated can help maintain the sacral chakra. You can also consider taking vitamin C supplements.

Essential Oils for the Sacral Chakra

The sacral chakra, associated with sensuality and pleasure, can benefit from the use of spicy essential oils. Sandalwood, which is useful for the root chakra, is also beneficial for the sacral chakra. You can also use orange oil. In order to stimulate sexual energy, many people swear by ylang-ylang, which is also reported to have a calming effect. This will help you relax and open up to pleasure. Clary sage is mildly spicy and found to be relaxing so that you will open your sensuality. It is particularly useful for older women. Also, consider using essential oils and lower back massage.

Colors for the Sacral Chakra

The sacral chakra is closely associated with deep, bright orange color. You can elevate your sensual energies by surrounding yourself with orange. Consider adding orange sheets, pillowcases, or bedspreads to the bedroom. Use orange pillows in your meditation space. You can also heighten your sexual energy by wearing bright orange-colored clothing items.

Crystals for the Sacral Chakra

The main crystal preferred for the sacral chakra is carnelian. This amazing stone, when polished, has the exact bright deep orange colors that activate the sacral chakra. Consider filling your bedroom with carnelian stones. Hold them in your hands, just for the sake of doing so or during meditation, and feel the energy and absorb it. Get a carnelian pendant or necklace to wear on your body to heighten your sensuality.

Amber is also a good crystal to use for the sacral chakra. It also overlaps with the solar plexus chakra, and you can use amber by purchasing jewelry items made of amber and wearing it on your body.

Goldstone is a dark orange crystal that can also help with the sacral chakra. Sunstone, tiger's eye, and citrine can also be used. However, note that these crystals are primarily yellow in color and have more impact on the solar plexus chakra. In summary, the carnelian stone is the primary crystal that you probably want to use to work on the sacral chakra.

Meditation for the Sacral Chakra

Meditation is going to be an important component for healing the sacral chakra. When you need to heal the sacral chakra, fill the meditation space with bright orange colors. If you can meditate during the day, especially in the morning hours, have open windows that allow a lot of sunlight into the room. Meditation for the sacral chakra will follow the basic pathway described in the last chapter. Begin by sitting in easy pose position and close your eyes, breathing deeply and regularly. When meditating for the sacral chakra, tuck your chin down a little bit to help open up the spine to increase energy flow. Some people even advise meditating nude or with little clothing when working on healing the sacral chakra so that you can feel the sensuality throughout the body. If you feel comfortable doing this and have the privacy to do so, it can really heighten the experience.

Begin by imagining a glowing white disk in front of you. Hold your breath for three to five seconds as you breathe. Start to see the disk rotating, slowly at first. As it rotates, see the disk gradually assume an orange color. Visualize the orange color gradually filling up the disk as it spins faster with time, generating more energy. Now, feel the ball of light enter your body, rising slowly and assuming a deeper and brighter orange color as it moves up to your root chakra. Keep visualizing it, and imagine the glowing disk fully assume a deep, bright, and energetic orange color. Now, visualize it moving to your sacral chakra region, below the navel.

Concentrate on your sacral chakra region and genital area. Be consciously aware of all the sensations, and in particular, feel sensations of heat as they arise. You can also visualize warming, glowing orange energy covering the area of the breasts. Do not be shy; healthy sexuality enjoys it to the fullest while maintaining natural control. The mediations will help you to arrive at this place in your life.

Now, imagine the orange disk rising into your brain. This will help elevate your creativity and have healthy fantasies that are not destructive and don't become obsessions. You can end the meditation at this point.

Affirmations for the Sacral Chakra

Using affirmations can help with the sacral chakra to help you achieve a healthy balance and to undo negative programming related to sexuality and sensuality.

• I strongly feel my emotions, but I am not overwhelmed by them.

• My emotions are strong and balanced.

• I feel relaxed and at peace.

• I am gifted with creativity.

• I experience creativity and am happy to share it with others.

- I allow my feelings to move through every pore in my body.

- I am comfortable with my body.

- I feel sensuality in my body.

- Sex is safe and allows me to form sacred connections.

- I am safe while enjoying sex.

- I radiate sexuality and sensuality.

- I allow myself to feel comfortable.

- I can enjoy pleasure without guilt.

- I am able to feel and enjoy all the pleasures life has to offer.

- My ability to enjoy good meals is heightened and intense.

- I attract like-minded people who are healthy in their sexuality.

- I can express my sexuality in healthy ways.

- I enjoy the passions life has to offer, without being overwhelmed by them.

Chapter 5 - Solar Plexus Chakra

As we move up the chakras, we move away from aspects of our being that are more "animal" and emotional in nature, and into more mature and eventually spiritually oriented characteristics. The solar plexus chakra possesses many of the characteristics we expect people to begin adopting in young adulthood and their teenage years. These characteristics are those that will help you in your workplace or help you excel in a school environment. Think of the solar plexus chakra as giving you self-confidence and willpower you need to get things done and take care of yourself and to take care of others as well.

The Solar Plexus Chakra Explained

The solar plexus chakra is found in the central abdominal area. It is above the navel and below the rib cage. Being higher energy than the root and sacral chakras, the solar plexus chakra is yellow in color. Keep in mind that we are talking about the spiritual aspects of energy. Certainly, as far as the energy you feel in your body, the energies of the sacral chakra can be quite intense. So the physical intensity of the experience is not the type of energy we are talking about when discussing the energy levels of the chakras. We are referring to the spiritual energy of vibration. Since the solar plexus chakra is involved in higher-level functioning than the root and sacral chakras, it has higher energy. Yellow vibrates at a higher frequency than orange light, which vibrates at a higher frequency than red light. The solar plexus chakra is represented by 10 lotus petals, and the element most commonly associated with the solar plexus chakra is fire. In Sanskrit, the solar plexus chakra is called **Manipura**.

Nonetheless, the solar plexus chakra is still a matter chakra. The reason is that the solar plexus chakra is going to be associated with earthly, rather than spiritual concerns, even if we can say they are more of an intellectual nature.

The main theme of the solar plexus chakra is empowerment. When you think of the solar plexus chakra, think of self-confidence in your interactions with others. While the solar plexus chakra is not specifically associated with work, it has a large influence on work and career. Those who are very successful in the work environment are going to have a strong and open solar plexus chakra.

When you have a healthy and open solar plexus chakra, you are going to have a strong sense of self-confidence in

47

the work environment or when you are working on projects with others, even if it's just a family project. If you have an open and healthy solar plexus chakra, taking the lead is something that comes naturally. You have the self-confidence to express the creative ideas that originate from the sacral chakra. You also take responsibility for your plans and actions.

In short, the solar plexus chakra can be associated with all the characteristics of a leader. Strong leaders from history, such as Catherine the Great, Napoleon, Patton, or Caesar, all had a strong and healthy solar plexus. Of course, how confidence and the ability to lead are actually used in practice depends on other factors. The solar plexus generates our confidence and willpower; it does not ensure that this is used for the good.

When you have a healthy solar plexus chakra, you are going to find that the ability to execute your plans comes with ease. Self-discipline is going to be a part of your personality without having to think about it. This also reflects the importance of balance. Someone who is out of balance, for example, with the sacral chakra, will lack the self-discipline that comes with the solar plexus. Often, in order to do hard work that is necessary to reach our career goals, self-discipline is necessary, which means putting off the pleasures of life until it is appropriate. When is that? You can engage in pleasures when it is not going to prevent you from achieving your professional goals.

While the root chakra is associated with the ability to meet your basic needs and fundamental financial security, wealth building is associated with the solar plexus chakra. This is because the ability to amass wealth is going to be dependent on being able to carry out your plans with confidence. You can get yellow carved stones in the shape of money trees to help the solar plexus chakra, and many people recommend this. Wealth and abundance are strongly associated with the solar plexus chakra.

It is possible to have a mindset of wealth and abundance at a job or career where you excel or as an independent thinking entrepreneur. You also don't have to be employed in the best job. The self-discipline of the person with a healthy solar plexus chakra means that they are able to save and invest money effectively and that they will do it over the time required to build their own personal wealth. Their self-confidence means that they are not going to compare their level of wealth to others. Instead, they will be happily amassing the level of wealth that is necessary for their own situation.

If you have a healthy solar plexus chakra, then you have a strong sense of direction in life and a sense of purpose when it comes to work and career, or maybe with respect to your role inside the home. You will be able to see things clearly and have reasoned judgment. Moreover, you will trust your own judgment and not question your decisions or be bothered by self-doubt.

If your solar plexus chakra is open and healthy, you are going to be confident about speaking up, and you will be the one that sets the direction and gets others to follow your lead. Although this does not apply in all cases, if you have a strong solar plexus chakra, you are going to have an intellectual side and have strong intellectual and analytical abilities. Even if you are more creative, when your solar plexus chakra is strong and healthy, you are going to have an intellectual and analytical side that enables you to turn your creativity into bold action that generates success. You can see this among creative types, such as authors, artists, or even people who enjoy working in the kitchen and making recipes. Have you noticed that many people absolutely excel at becoming authors or artists? And then there are those who are the perennial "starving artist" or a writer who is always writing but never completing projects or lacking the ability to get them published. You also see people starting recipe sites and becoming minor celebrities; they are able to transform their passion for cooking and coming up with recipes into a full-time living online.

The linkage between the sacral chakra and the solar plexus chakra in this regard cannot be underestimated. You can focus on this to determine the health of your own solar plexus chakra, assuming that your sacral chakra is open or at least reasonably functioning. Are you having lots of creative ideas and plans that seem to fail to materialize? Or are your ideas something that you find easy to actually implement?

If you have a healthy solar plexus chakra, you will be confident and strong in your beliefs and opinions. This does not mean being pushy about them. People who are pushy with their beliefs often betray inner insecurity. When plagued by insecurity, you are likely to have a problem getting spun up and emotional when challenged on your beliefs or when you are presented with opinions that differ from your own. Someone with a healthy solar plexus chakra is going to be a person who has an inner confidence and calm, and who lets this confidence shine through when challenged, without getting emotional or belittling others.

If your solar plexus chakra is open, you are going to find that things are nearly effortless. That doesn't mean that you do not have to put in hard work or devote energy to your projects but that your efforts will flow naturally. People with a healthy solar plexus chakra seem to know on an intuitive level what they need to do in order to plan and carry out any endeavor. They may also exude a high level of energy that is contagious to others.

How the Solar Plexus Chakra Gets Blocked?

Events that sap our confidence in childhood can lead to a blocked solar plexus chakra. In many cases, it can be a guardian or teacher, who while meaning well, use harsh language and put-downs trying to motivate children to work harder. Often, instead of helping the child, they sap the child's self-confidence, leaving them with low self-esteem and taking away their natural can-do attitude.

Of course, you don't have to be a child to be affected by this. Anytime someone important to you engages in put-downs or doubts your abilities, you might start to feel a lack of self-confidence. The energy that is associated with this kind of self-doubt is going to lead to a blockage of the solar plexus chakra.

Depending on the overall balance of the chakras and the makeup of the person, the inevitable failures that happen in life can have a large impact on the solar plexus chakra. If you are coming from a place of strength, to begin with, you can bounce back from failures easily. If all three of the lower chakras (root, sacral, and solar plexus) are open, and in balance, a failure on a major project is going to lead to analysis and planning to recover from the failure and learn lessons that can be applied next time. But if you are already suffering from blockages or imbalance, a failure on a project can serve to fully block your solar plexus chakra.

Also, the reactions of those around us can determine how we respond to failure, whether it is on a work project, something in the home, or at school. There are many negative people in the world who will use the failure of someone else to put them down. If you are the recipient of this kind of behavior, it can help to block the solar plexus chakra.

Symptoms of a Solar Plexus Chakra Blockage

For the most part, when you think of symptoms of a solar plexus chakra, think of the opposite of what we have discussed so far. While a person with an open and functioning solar plexus chakra will be brimming with self-confidence and be eager to take on and complete projects, if you have a blocked solar plexus chakra, you are probably going to be the quiet person in the corner, who avoids taking on too much responsibility. You might have problems completing projects, plagued by self-doubt. You might lack the confidence to speak out and voice your opinions. Being unsure of yourself, you might not even have firm opinions and beliefs.

When you have a blocked solar plexus chakra, you might have a poverty mentality. Having a poverty mentality doesn't necessarily mean that you are living in a rundown apartment, or even having trouble making ends meet. However, it means you will not think in terms of wealth and abundance. You will have a strong belief that the amount of money you have now is all that you can attain, and that wealth and riches are a matter of "luck." This mindset will keep you from taking action that could change your financial situation. Instead, you will be satisfied with the status quo, thinking that this is just the "way it is." Often, a poverty mentality is related to a blocked root chakra as well, and there is a belief (in some cases, existing at the level of the subconscious) that you will never have enough money.

If you have a blocked solar plexus chakra, you will lack the self-discipline needed to be a leader who gets things done. You will find that at the first opportunity, you will abandon any hard work for the chance to engage in pleasurable activities. If you are engaged in any creative projects, you'll have an inability to bring them to completion. The person with a healthy sacral chakra but a blocked solar plexus often has several half-completed projects lying around. They never seem to be able to "close the deal," and they are completely unable to lead others where they need to go.

An inability to maintain boundaries can often arise in this case. This comes from a lack of self-discipline, and it becomes difficult to maintain levels of hard work. Entrepreneurs who are successful have a strong level of self-discipline because they need to separate work from "play" in order to achieve success. If you have a blocked solar plexus, this might be something that is very difficult for you, and you find you are never getting anywhere as a result.

Apathy and Lack of Purpose

Two qualities that are often associated with a blocked solar plexus are apathy and lack of purpose. The degree of apathy will vary from person to person, but when the solar plexus chakra is blocked, you can become pretty apathetic about having to work and your work life in general. While in school, you might find yourself unable to see anything satisfying or something you could get passionate about. People with a blocked solar plexus chakra that go to college often jump around from major to major. They do so because no matter what they try, they feel apathetic about it, and they also lack the discipline to stick to something and take it to completion. Don't be surprised if they fail to graduate. If they do graduate, it will be from muddling through, not because they have found something that engages their passions.

This is coupled with a general sense that there is a lack of purpose in life. This can also be accompanied by blockages at the spiritual levels. However, when the solar plexus chakra is blocked, there will be a lack of purpose that relates to a sense of occupation or career. This will be accompanied by a lack of caring for work or efforts at work, and the person will do what is necessary to get by and avoid getting fired, but nothing more.

An Overactive Solar Plexus

Just like we've seen with the sacral chakra, it is possible to be out of balance and have an overactive solar plexus chakra as well. In this case, the workaholic personality comes to mind. Some people have an overactive solar plexus and so devote too much time to work and earning money. They will put in excessive hours at the office and won't balance that out with meeting their normal human needs for pleasure and relaxation. They will always find an excuse to stay late at the office. If they have a partner or family at home, this is going to be the person who neglects their family. They may also neglect their health, working so much that they develop ulcers, digestive problems, and even serious health problems like heart disease and cancer.

Surprisingly, people with an overactive solar plexus chakra are penny pinchers. Since the solar plexus chakra can be associated with a mentality of wealth and abundance, when it is overactive and out of balance, this can lead to valuing money for its own sake. The person becomes unwilling to spend any money, even for reasonable expenses. Despite a high income, they become obsessed with saving a penny at every turn. They will use coupons, refuse to lend anyone money, and drive an old, beat-up car. They will be severely judgmental of people who enjoy luxury items or take vacations. This is the type of person who, if they never heal, will take their money to the grave with them.

Food for the Solar Plexus Chakra

Yellow, brightly colored foods can help heal the solar plexus chakra. Start with squash. Flavor your foods and your drinks with lemon. Add yellow peppers to your salads. Eat corn, tacos with yellow corn shells, or corn chips. Golden apples will help to open the solar plexus chakra. You can also help the solar plexus chakra by eating pasta, lentils, and oats. Regular potatoes can help as well, and use lots of butter, especially grass-fed butter that will have a strong, deep yellow color.

Essential Oils for the Solar Plexus Chakra

The top essential oil to use for healing the solar plexus is lemon oil. Many other oils can be helpful, however. These include chamomile, ginger, and cinnamon oil. Some practitioners that use essential oils also advise clove oil for the solar plexus chakra.

Colors for the Solar Plexus Chakra

Of course, bright yellow colors are good for healing the solar plexus chakra. You can also combine yellow and white. Fill your life with these colors, and let as much sunshine into your living space as possible, especially in the mornings, late afternoon, or early evening as sunset approaches. Use yellow sheets on your bed and yellow pillows and consider painting a room bright yellow to use for meditation on the solar plexus chakra when necessary.

Crystals for the Solar Plexus Chakra

There are several yellow-colored crystals and stones that can be used to help you heal the solar plexus chakra. Among the most popular is a crystal called citrine. Some stones used to heal the sacral chakra overlap with the solar plexus chakra, and utilizing them can help you to heal both at the same time and bring them into balance. Try using amber for this purpose, and the tiger's eye also works well for both chakras. Other stones that can help you heal the solar plexus chakra include yellow jasper and yellow topaz.

Meditation for the Solar Plexus Chakra

To meditate for the solar plexus chakra, assume the easy pose position and close your eyes, breathing deeply. Meditating in the morning hours or at sunset can be very helpful for the solar plexus chakra, especially if you can meditate outside or by a window where you can sit in the sunlight. The sun's energy is yellow, so it is highly attuned to the solar plexus chakra. But don't worry if meditating in the sun isn't practical for you.

During the meditation, see a spinning wheel of bright yellow light. While meditating for the solar plexus chakra, you will want this disk of light to pass through the root and sacral chakras on its journey. Try to see the disk of light grow brighter and more energetic as it rises up into the location of the solar plexus chakra. When you breathe in, see the disk expand in size, and then see it shrink as you breathe out. Meditate on this chakra for about 15 minutes per day.

As I said earlier, if you are able to meditate in the sun during the morning hours or toward sunset, this can be very helpful. You can feel and absorb the warming energy of the sun's yellow light as you meditate.

Affirmations for the Solar Plexus Chakra

So much that is associated with the solar plexus chakra takes place on a subconscious level; daily affirmations can be especially helpful in this case. Use the following to help you get started.

- I am strong and confident.

- I will finish anything that I start.

- I am a leader, and I am comfortable setting the direction of others.

- I deserve to have my ideas heard.

- I am a creative being, and I can turn my visions into reality.

- I feel awakened by the sun's powerful yellow energy.

- I will channel the powerful yellow energy of the sun into a creative purpose.

- I rejoice at my ability to make things happen.

- I believe in my own abilities and feel strong and independent.

- My body is full of the energy I need to complete all my projects.

- I can establish plans and turn them into reality.

- I am full of personal power.
- I am smart and have clear judgment.
- I can express my will without harming others.
- I am able to accurately evaluate any situation.
- I am a leader and a decision-maker.
- I am a master of my own life.
- I am attracting wealth and abundance.

Chapter 6 - Heart Chakra

In this chapter, we begin our journey into the spiritual realm. Here, we meet the heart chakra. Technically speaking, this is not considered to be a spiritual chakra, and some consider it to be intermediate, linking together the matter chakras and the spiritual chakras. The heart chakra is associated with love, acceptance, and empathy. Of course, these types of emotions and states of being cross many boundaries. In some ways, romantic love is a very primitive emotion. Many people experience romantic love, but it's in an immature state. If that's the case, although they have feelings for another person, romantic love is actually self-directed, and in some cases, it can even be selfish. In the immature state, romantic love can often mean possession of another person. But when you haven't reached a certain level of growth and maturity, of course, it's true that romantic love can mean loving somebody more than yourself and coming together as a union.

> Therefore, we see that heart chakra involves both the physical and the spiritual when looking at the situation of romantic love. The emotional components can be primitive and ego-based, but they can also be selfless in nature.

This indicates that the heart chakra encompasses both matter and spirit. It has many aspects that go well beyond romantic love. In order to develop those aspects and fully unleash the potential of the heart chakra, you must heal the root chakra, the sacral chakra, and the solar plexus chakra first.

At its fundamental level, the heart chakra involves a love of self and self-acceptance. The emotions of empathy, tolerance, and understanding of others come from the heart chakra. So, we see that the power of the heart chakra involves love and understanding of all humanity and, indeed all of life itself.

What Is the Heart Chakra?

The heart chakra is located in the center of the chest. The color of the heart chakra is green, which is a very appropriate color and energy level. The green color indicates the heart chakra is vibrating at a higher frequency as compared to the solar plexus and the lower chakras. It can also involve pink colors when vibrating at specific frequencies, and you might guess that these energetic frequencies are more in tune with romantic love. In Sanskrit, the name of the heart chakra is Anahata. The heart chakra is depicted as a green flower with 12 lotus petals.

A healthy heart chakra begins with the love of self. If you don't love yourself, you are not going to be able to share the love with others, and truly love others. When you truly love other people, satisfying their needs is as important, if not more so, than satisfying your own. The heart chakra is certainly associated with love, relationships, and friendship. The most intensity felt with the heart chakra is often when you are in romantic love, and many people will get strong sensations, even pain, in the center of their chest when romantic love is involved.

However, the heart chakra is also associated with "platonic" forms of love. The love of your children, which is unconditional and, therefore, strongly associated with green colors, is a function of the heart chakra. The love experienced in friendship also comes from the heart chakra, although the intensity may be lower. Love of pets and animals also comes from the heart chakra.

There is also a genuine love, compassion, and empathy; most of us feel for all people and living things. Although this type of love has a different character, our compassion for others, indeed for all life, also comes from the heart chakra.

The heart chakra goes well beyond this, however. There are many characteristics and emotions associated with the heart chakra that can operate at a higher level. We will also come to understand the heart chakra better when we understand all of the chakras because the heart chakra is often described as a linkage point that connects the matter chakras to the spiritual chakras. For this reason, the state of the heart chakra can play a role in how you deal with and recover from illnesses and setbacks in life. When the heart chakra is open and healed, you find it easier to deal with stress, and if you do suffer from illness, you will find that you recover faster. In turn, things like illness and stress, if unchecked, can negatively impact the heart chakra.

The painful loss of a loved one gives rise to the strong emotion of grief. As a part of grief, we have to come to terms with our loss and reach a state of peace. The heart chakra plays a central role in this process, both in the ability to feel and express grief and also in our ability to come to terms with it. Those who have developed spiritually have an awareness that life goes on without the physical body, so they also have an easier time coming to terms with the grief of physical loss.

While the root, sacral, and solar plexus can be thought of as "me" chakras, the heart chakra can be thought of as a chakra that establishes a connection. The heart chakra allows the exchange of energy with other life that is around you, from the smallest flower to people and spirit. When your heart chakra is open and healed, you will find that relating to others is easy, and your relationships are harmonious and without difficulty.

The heart chakra also helps you to integrate all of your thoughts and emotions and brings you closer to the idea of wisdom rather than mere creativity. As such, when your heart chakra is open, the creativity that arises from the sacral chakra reaches a much higher level of significance.

The heart chakra can also have a big influence on the solar plexus chakra. While the solar plexus chakra by itself can help you feel confident and be a decisive leader, an open heart chakra is necessary to be a good leader. This is because an open heart chakra is going to help you feel empathy and compassion for others. You will be able to take others' ideas and feelings into account. A leader who has an open heart chakra is one that will build a team where everyone feels like they are an important contributor.

The appreciation of beauty comes from the heart chakra as well. With the sacral chakra, we have the appreciation of pleasure and of luxury. But it is the heart chakra that elevates this to a higher level. If you are able to appreciate the paintings of Rembrandt or good music, then you have a developed and open heart chakra.

When you have an open heart chakra, you live a carefree existence, and you always come from a place of empathy and compassion. You find it easy to feel and establish a connection with others. Building bridges comes easily to you when your heart chakra is open. You trust others, and they trust you. It is easy for you to give to other people, and you never feel a loss from it. In fact, when the heart chakra is opened, you will feel the good and positive energy from giving.

When the heart chakra is open, romantic relationships come easily, and they are free of drama, jealousy, and hurt. While conflicts arise from time to time, resolving arguments is easy.

Acceptance and forgiveness are critical indicators of a heart chakra that is healthy. When your heart chakra is open, you are able to forgive others without issue, and your forgiveness is genuine. Here is another example where balance is key. The solar plexus chakra is going to be involved in not letting people exploit you or walk all over you. So, you need to be in balance with both the solar plexus and heart chakras so that your place of forgiveness does not put you in a position to be exploited by others. You can be tolerant and forgiving of other people, but not when they fail to show change or improvement.

"Connection" is the word that you can associate with the heart chakra. The element that is associated with the heart chakra is air. This characterizes the free flow of love energy among living beings, and we all share the air that we breathe, which is symbolic of the interconnectedness of all living things.

Being able to change is also a part of the heart chakra. When it is healthy, you are not stuck in your ways but are able to change and adapt, and even undergo a transformation when necessary.

How the Heart Chakra Gets Blocked?

There are many ways that the heart chakra can become blocked. When love is sporadic or withheld in childhood, this can block the heart chakra. Children can develop a blocked heart chakra if one parent abandons the family. While a divorce can be a traumatic experience for a child, it will not have lasting damage on the heart chakra if the other parent remains loving and involved in the child's life.

Any type of rejection throughout life can block the heart chakra. The younger and less developed you are, the more likely a blockage is going to occur. Rejection by friends can have a major impact on the heart chakra, especially if this occurs between the ages of 6-13. Of course, a failure to be accepted in the teenage years can also block the heart chakra.

When there is a rejection that is based on betrayal, the impact is especially important. At any age, when there is an experience of betrayal, the heart chakra can be blocked. This is something that occurs in romantic relationships, of course, but it can also happen in work relationships or among friends. Anything that removes the ability to trust others and, hence, limits the possible connectivity between yourself and others can block the heart chakra.

Again, the general pattern is that the younger you are when you experience betrayal, the more likely the heart chakra is to be blocked. However, this can happen at any age, as we have noted.

Like the other chakras, balance is very important when discussing the heart chakra. An out of balance heart chakra can lead to dysfunctional behaviors, and this can be just as important as a blocked heart chakra depending on the circumstances.

Symptoms of a Heart Chakra Blockage

The symptoms of a blocked heart chakra will be related to your feelings of connectivity and your ability to establish and maintain relationships of all kinds. Don't limit yourself by only thinking about romantic relationships when you are considering the heart chakra. The heart chakra is going to impact your ability to form connections with your parents, your siblings, your friends, humanity, generally, and with pet animals.

When the heart chakra is blocked because of bad experiences or rejections during childhood and adolescence, in adulthood, this can manifest strongly as social anxiety. If you are a very shy person, your heart chakra may have been blocked during the formative years of ages 3-8 or during the emotionally intense teenage years. Don't despair if you feel that you may have experienced this; a blocked heart chakra can be opened and healed.

Awareness is the first step to healing so that you can take corrective action.

Those who have a blocked heart chakra can manifest it in different ways. Some people will feel lonely and disconnected. Others may be resentful, unforgiving, and holding grudges. When you have a blocked chakra, you may be unable to feel empathy and compassion, and you might be very self-centered in your dealings and relationships with others. When this is the case, people may still get involved in romantic relationships and have a lot of social contacts. However, their view of these relationships will always be "what does this relationship do for **me**." This also indicates that there may be blockages on the higher chakras because there is a lack of spiritual development.

When there is a blockage of the heart chakra of this type, this can result in a state of jealousy and anger. There is also a lack of self-confidence that may be manifesting because of a blocked or underdeveloped solar plexus chakra. A person may be able to get involved in romantic relationships under these circumstances and feel intense emotions. However, this person's mind will always be filled with paranoid thoughts and a desire to always check up on his/her romantic partner. The slightest indication can set off feelings of jealousy and anger. Fear and suspicion of cheating or a feeling that the other person simply doesn't love you back are going to be prominent. This is going to be the case even if the other party is showing love.

Some people that have a blocked heart chakra will express it through the opposite of empathy. In these cases, they will adopt a highly judgmental and critical stance with respect to other people. They will lack compassion and are unlikely to donate to charity. In the work environment, they will view themselves as superior to others.

A blocked heart chakra can inhibit your ability to give freely to others. If you do give and share with others, you will be doing it, expecting something in return. Or you will be doing it with the expectation of acknowledgment so that you can use the act of giving, not for the benefit of helping others, but to enhance your own self-esteem and how you appear to others.

In many cases, a blocked heart chakra will lead people to be closed off and reserved. They may completely abstain from romantic relationships. If the blockage is particularly severe, they will have few friends, and they will only rarely socialize with them. They may even avoid immediate family. Some people develop a blocked heart chakra when their parents die and, afterward, find that they are withdrawing from other family members and even friends. In some cases, the only social contact these people get is from work.

A blocked heart chakra can also result in many physical symptoms. These can include indigestion and heartburn, high blood pressure, chest pains, and shoulder pains. Even heart disease can result in serious cases, and medical doctors admit that social disconnection can lead to heart disease. Since chest pains can be a symptom of heart trouble, please see your doctor in case you need immediate treatment.

An Overactive Heart Chakra

Previously, we have seen that an overactive chakra can be as damaging as a blocked chakra. In the case of the sacral chakra, we saw that an overactive sacral chakra could lead to problems, such as sexual addiction, drinking, drug use, and gambling.

An overactive heart chakra can also be damaging. When

the heart chakra is out of balance, like the sacral chakra, we can see the aspects of the heart chakra expressed at an excessive level.

Let's think about the emotion of love and caring for others. There is a balance that is achieved between the ego/self and the other person. This is true, no matter what type of love we are talking about. In a healthy relationship, you do not only care about the needs of the other person, but you also care about your own needs. Assuming that you have appropriate levels of self-confidence, you will make your own needs known to your partner or friend. We also know that there is a balance, and compromise is an important part of healthy relationships.

This boundary between the self and the other can melt away and vanish when the heart chakra is overactive. In severe cases, people lose their entire sense of identity. When this happens, you may not work to satisfy your own needs at all, and instead, you will be completely attending to the needs of others. You can loosely think of this as being completely selfless, or having a "Mother Theresa" complex. While many people admire those, like Mother Theresa, who devoted their lives to giving to others, the truth is, for most of us, it is an unhealthy way to approach interpersonal relationships. Loving humanity at the complete expense of yourself is not a way to contribute either.

Others with an overactive heart chakra are not quite that dramatic. But they will find that they are constantly getting involved in co-dependent relationships. Healthy adults do not base their relationships on co-dependency, and instead, both contribute to the needs of the other, and each can take care of themselves independently. A relationship that is healthy is bringing together two independent souls to form something that is greater than the sum of their parts.

In a co-dependent relationship, you essentially have a needy child and a person with an overactive heart chakra who ends up playing the role of a parent figure. A large part of the relationship will be based on the person with the overactive heart chakra, supporting the needs of the other person, without having their own needs satisfied.

Another symptom of an overactive heart chakra is being too willing to trust people. We have seen that a blockage can result when trust is betrayed, and trust plays an important role in establishing connections with other people. But the reality of the world is that there are a lot of people out there who are not worthy of trust. They will steal, cheat, and hurt other people. When you lack proper discernment, you will find yourself getting into relationships of this type, and it will cost you in many ways. Often, a person with an overactive heart chakra is going to be too willing to trust and accept people, and they will suffer as a result when people not worthy of trust get intimately involved in their lives and end up taking and destroying.

This brings us to another aspect of someone with an overactive chakra. When your heart chakra is overactive, you are going to say yes to everything. You might find that you are always giving other people money, even when it ends up hurting you. Or you might never properly meet your own needs for health, exercise, and **me** time because you are always saying yes to anyone. Although this can affect people of both genders, women tend to be the "yes" people more often than men do.

Another indicator of an overactive heart chakra is that you are constantly and easily getting involved in love relationships. You might find yourself "falling in love" frequently and then jumping from person to person. When the heart chakra is open but healthy and balanced, you should not fall in love easily. You will be open to love, but you will also be discriminating and careful.

The bottom line with an overactive heart chakra is that it is going to be associated with the complete erosion of the ego and self.

Foods for the Heart Chakra

Green colored foods are very helpful for the heart chakra. You can eat green vegetables, including spinach, broccoli, and green beans. You can also use olive oil and eat avocados. Green olives are also good, along with green peppers. Basically, any green vegetables can be included in your meals for this purpose, and kiwi is a green fruit, along with lime, which can help heal the heart chakra. Think of innovative ways to incorporate lime into your diet. Highly energetic foods can also help, including types of meat that are pinkish. With this in mind, consider salmon. Pork can also be consumed for this purpose, and you can also eat prime rib.

Essential Oils for the Heart Chakra

When thinking about healing the heart chakra, think about igniting compassion and connection. Rose oil can be used to help you expand and develop the heart chakra. The pleasant scent of rose oil will help to open up the heart and bring about feelings of joy and empathy, as well as promoting a feeling of calm. Neroli oil with its citrus scents will help you establish a fundamental baseline for the heart chakra, helping to open it while keeping you from losing your sense of self. Marjoram, with its green colors, is also a good essential oil to use for healing when traumatic events may have blocked your heart chakra.

Colors for the Heart Chakra

The colors you want to surround yourself with to heal the heart chakra are shades of green. You can use various tones of green, and it can be helpful to wear green items of clothing and green crystals (see below). You can use green pillows, drapes, and sheets to promote the green energy that is associated with the heart chakra.

Crystals for the Heart Chakra

Many crystals can be used with the heart chakra, including the green emerald and jade. The choice of color can be based on what aspects of the heart chakra are giving you the most trouble. If the problem is general in nature, stick to naturally green-colored stones. If it is primarily romantic love giving you problems, you can use rose quartz to promote healing.

Meditation for the Heart Chakra

The meditation for the heart chakra will focus on green colors. As usual, assume the easy pose position. Imagine a green ball of light coming toward you. See it growing large, getting as large as you are, and positioned right in front of you. Now, each time you breathe in, see the green light enter through your nose and fill your entire chest energy. When you do this, feel the energy of love, connection, trust, and empathy that the green energy carries with it. See yourself breathing in the green light for 15-20 minutes. Each time, hold your breath for a count of five seconds.

Affirmations for the Heart Chakra

Affirmations for the heart chakra can help you to restore your proper sense of self and the confidence to enter into healthy, loving relationships.

- I feel love and connection with other human beings.

- I trust others, but they must earn my trust.

- I deserve to be loved and respected.

- I love socializing and being with family and friends.

- I will give freely to others without expecting anything in return.

- I will help others but not at the expense of causing me pain.

- The love I feel for all life is boundless and filled with joy.

- I am open to giving love to others.

- I forgive myself for the mistakes I have made.

- I love myself unconditionally.

- I am open to receiving love.

- I forgive others completely and unconditionally.

- I am compassionate for others and the suffering they may be experiencing.

- I will devote a portion of my life to helping others after I have met my own needs first.

Chapter 7 - Throat Chakra

The throat chakra is the first truly spiritual chakra. You should not work on the throat chakra until you have healed and brought all the other chakras that we have talked about into balance. So before attending to the throat chakra, please work on healing the root, sacral, solar plexus, and heart chakras.

What Is the Throat Chakra?

The throat chakra is located in the front and lower part of the throat. Think of the throat chakra's location as the area where speech originates in your throat. The

Sanskrit name of the throat chakra is **Vishuddha**. The color that is associated with the throat chakra is blue. Often, it is depicted as a shade of aquamarine or turquoise. Indeed, turquoise is an excellent stone to use in crystal work with the throat chakra.

The blue color reflects the higher vibrational energy of this spiritual chakra with respect to the other chakras we have studied so far. Scientists tell us that blue light is higher energy than green light, which is higher energy than yellow light, and so on. The more spiritual you get, the higher the energy of vibration, so the spiritual chakras are colored in the blue to purple range. The heart chakra, being a linkage point between the matter and spiritual chakras, and involving aspects that are matter and spirit, is green, which reflects a mixture of blue and yellow energies.

Another way that higher energy states are represented is the number of petals on the flower used to represent the chakra. In the case of the throat chakra, there are sixteen lotus petals.

When we get to the spiritual chakras, they are more sophisticated due to their spiritual nature. First, let's take a moment to talk about the dimensionality of the universe. Our physical universe is four-dimensional, with three physical dimensions for physical movement and one dimension of time. But scientists tell us that there are probably 11, 13, or even 26 dimensions. In these higher dimensions, we find psychic and spiritual energies, and this is likely where those who have passed on reside.

The point of this is that the throat chakra is located in the throat area, but being a spiritual chakra, it actually extends slightly outside of your body.

The key to the throat chakra is information, truth, and

communication. The spiritual aspect of the throat chakra is that it connects your inner spirit with the material, physical world. You use your voice to translate your inner thoughts and ideas so that they can be expressed to others. So, in this sense, the throat chakra helps us to establish a connection with other people. This is true, no matter what type of interaction we are describing. When you are involved in a romantic or sexual relationship, you need to be able to communicate your thoughts and feelings. This is where the throat chakra interacts and interplays with the heart and sacral chakras. Furthermore, you need to be able to communicate your ideas for creativity or at work. In this way, the throat chakra interacts with the solar plexus chakra and the sacral chakra.

The throat chakra will also be involved in your relationships with people in any context, so it will be closely tied to the heart chakra.

One of the most important aspects of the throat chakra is being able to speak the truth. This is the truth and your truth. It is also involved in your ability to speak out to others when appropriate. The throat chakra is closely associated with any kind of communication, including nonverbal communication. With regard to the solar plexus, where we saw that an open solar plexus chakra is important for being able to turn your creative ideas into reality, the throat chakra is important as well. This is because of its role in communication. If you cannot communicate your ideas with others and do so in a truthful manner, you are not going to see your ideas realized.

A sense of purpose is closely tied to the throat chakra as well. When it comes to purpose in the sense of work and career, this is another aspect where the throat chakra is integrated with the solar plexus. Opening the throat chakra will make your communications with others more effective, so it is an important aspect of bringing together your creativity, drive, and vision.

How the Throat Chakra Gets Blocked?

Experiences that are negative with respect to communicating your truth or ideas can result in a throat chakra blockage. Again, if this happens in childhood or adolescence, the impact is going to be strongly felt. If parents or guardians mock a child when the child comes to them with ideas or the truth, this can be very damaging and work to block the throat chakra. As you get older, the throat chakra can become blocked if people mock or disregard your thoughts and ideas. That can be a potent weapon used by those who are abusive.

Symptoms of a Throat Chakra Blockage

A throat chakra blockage is going to manifest in problems communicating with others. This can happen in multiple ways. For example, you may be too shy to speak in groups or to reveal your true feelings and needs in intimate situations. If you feel that you have an inappropriate fear of talking, this should be taken as a symptom of blockage in your throat chakra. This can occur in groups of people in social situations, in one-on-one situations, or in work situations. This type of blockage may also be related to a blocked solar plexus chakra since the solar plexus is associated with self-confidence, so please take this into account as well. In those cases, it is appropriate to meditate on both chakras.

Another way that a blockage of the throat chakra can manifest is that you speak in low volumes. Do you find that people say that they can't hear what you are saying? Or maybe people can't hear you speak at all. In cases like this, people with the throat chakra blockage feel as though people are ignoring them when the reality is that people are not even aware they are speaking. Often, this happens in social situations of three or more people or in the work environment. The feeling of being ignored can cause the throat chakra blockage to lead to other blockages. It will create new anxieties in social situations that can weaken or block the heart chakra. The feeling of being ignored when you are trying to voice your ideas may make you feel less valued, and it can lower your self-esteem and self-confidence, leading to a blocked solar plexus chakra. In a sense, the throat chakra is an important chakra when it comes to our interactions with others and our perceptions of these interactions, so blockage of the throat chakra can lead to a cascade of blockage among many chakras.

Conversely, the throat chakra is also impacted by the health of the solar plexus chakra and the heart chakra. If you are lacking in confidence or feeling socially disconnected, this will weaken the throat chakra, even if it is open, leading to possible blockages as things develop.

It's important to note that a blocked throat chakra does not just impact your ability to speak. In fact, the worst effect of a blocked throat chakra is its negative impact on your character. Another is how your character is revealed through your speech habits. For example, people who are chronic liars are usually people who have a blocked throat chakra. This is because the throat chakra is closely tied to the ability to speak the truth.

Keeping your word is also an important personality characteristic that is closely related to the throat chakra. If you are not able to keep your word, people cannot trust you, and what you say, promise, or make deals on cannot be trusted. Most people would argue this is a severe character flaw. If your throat chakra is blocked, then you are more likely to engage in behavior of this sort, where you say one thing and do another, or make agreements with people and don't keep them.

Other character flaws that indicate a blocked throat chakra include being prone to gossip or being unable to keep a secret. If you are someone who reveals deep truths about others or has to spread rumors about people, and you feel like this is an impulsive behavior, a blockage of the throat chakra is likely a result of these types of actions.

Mumbling while speaking is also a classic symptom of a throat chakra that is blocked. In this case, your voice may be loud enough, but you are subconsciously altering the use of your mouth and tongue in ways that are dysfunctional so that other people cannot understand the content of your speech.

A tendency to "say the wrong thing" can also be an indication of throat chakra that is blocked. This can also manifest as saying something that is okay generally but inappropriate for the moment.

Another way that a blocked throat chakra can manifest in ways that are related to character issues is using speech to put down others or make them feel bad.

A blockage in the throat chakra impacts all types of communication. So you may be saying these things in writing, not just vocalizing them. Writing is really just a different form of speaking, so what you write and whether your words on paper, emails, or text messages are genuine or not can be impacted by a blocked throat chakra.

Another interesting way that a blocked throat chakra can

impact people's behavior occurs when the throat chakra is overactive. When it is overactive, a person may become a loud, boisterous speaker. We are all familiar with the overconfident loudmouth. In these cases, the person is either hiding underlying insecurities by speaking loudly and acting out in obnoxious ways, or they have an overactive throat chakra that leads them to communicate in ways that make them the center of attention while shutting down the ability of others to communicate.

This can also reveal itself in an inability to listen to others. You may have been in a relationship with someone that never "heard" what you are saying when voicing your feelings, or you may have a superior in a work environment who doesn't listen to your ideas or concerns. In these cases, a blocked throat chakra can be the cause, but often, an overactive throat chakra can lead these people to devalue the thoughts and opinions of others. An overactive throat chakra can even inhibit the ability of the person to even have a conscious awareness that others are communicating with them.

When doing a self-examination to see where you need to work on your chakras, don't be afraid to confront your own flaws. When you are reading about these personality characteristics, don't worry if you see yourself in them. It doesn't mean you are a bad person. It just means that you have to work to get better. Remember that in many cases, a blocked chakra is the result of the behavior of parents, guardians, and other caregivers when you were young, so you shouldn't be looking at a blocked chakra as indicating something is your fault. In any case, the fact that you are looking to study the chakras and willing to take action by taking up activities like meditation and yoga indicates that you are on the right path toward healing.

Physical Symptoms of a Blocked Throat Chakra

Physical symptoms of a blocked throat chakra are typically centered on causing difficulties speaking. Laryngitis is a common problem among those with a blocked throat chakra. Sore throats, often that cannot be traced to a specific cause, are also tied to a blocked throat chakra. A scratchy or dry throat often manifests when there is a blocked throat chakra, and you might feel like you always have to clear your throat. Neck pain or oral problems can also take place as a result. Recurrent biting of the tongue, creating discomfort, and soreness can be related to a blocked throat chakra. Dental problems, including toothaches, are also a possible symptom. Sometimes, the problem may not be in the immediate area, but rather in chronic sinus problems or allergies that can make communicating more difficult. You might even have pains in your hands or wrists, as these can make it difficult to type on a computer or send text messages.

In general, any problem that makes it more difficult to speak or to speak with a voice loud and clear enough for others to understand what you are saying, especially if this is a chronic or recurrent problem, is probably a symptom of a throat chakra that is blocked. When serious physical problems manifest, you should consult a medical doctor to take care of the immediate problem, but then you should work on the throat chakra to deal with the long-term energetic problems that are leading to the blockage and then causing these issues to develop in the first place.

Foods for the Throat Chakra

There are many foods that are useful for healing the throat chakra and maintaining its health. You are going to want to look for foods that are bluish in color, but purple-colored foods work as well. Blueberries and blackberries are excellent foods that can help to heal the throat chakra, besides the general health benefits that they provide. Dark-colored grapes of any shade can also help to heal the throat chakra. There are also purple varieties of potatoes that can be included in your diet as a part of the healing process for the throat chakra.

Essential Oils for the Throat Chakra

When using essential oils to heal the throat chakra, choose varieties that are calming and helpful for sore throats. You should also choose varieties that can help maintain and enhance your sense of well-being. Geranium is a good choice, as this citrusy oil is often used for sore throats. Jasmine oil can also be a good selection. Jasmine has been known to help with problems related to a hoarse voice. Many people have problems with hoarseness when they have a blocked throat chakra. Consider using jasmine oil if you have chronic problems with a hoarse voice.

One consideration with essential oils when working on healing the throat chakra is that you should take into account the fact that the throat chakra is a spiritual chakra, with a relatively high level of energetic vibration. Frankincense is a good oil to use with healing the throat chakra due to its elevated energetic frequency and its role as a spiritual and holy oil.

Colors for the Throat Chakra

Blue and aquamarine colors are associated with the throat chakra. Turquoise is also an excellent color that will help you to heal the throat chakra. When you are working on healing the throat chakra, you can decorate your home in varying shades of blue, from light to darker blues. The darker the shade of blue and the lower the level of green components in the coloring, the more spiritual the energy is. So, you might want to choose your shades appropriately, using darker colors if you feel that a blocked throat chakra is manifesting more in character issues like gossiping, lying, or not keeping your word. If your blocked throat chakra is manifesting in insecurities while speaking, or keeping things to yourself that you want or need to communicate to others, opt for more light shades and include colors of blue that are mixtures of blues and greens, such as aquamarine and turquoise. For most people, when you are working on healing the throat chakra, a mixture of these colors is preferred so that you can have a healing energy that will help with all aspects of your consciousness related to the throat chakra.

You can also wear blue colors while working on healing the throat chakra. Wear blue colors when meditating or doing yoga, and you can also wear blue colors throughout the day.

Crystals for the Throat Chakra

Many good crystals are available for helping to heal the throat chakra, and due to their vibrant and pleasing colors, they make good jewelry items that can be worn to help promote the energetic frequency of an open throat chakra. As with the colors that you wear or fill your home with, you can select different varieties of stones and crystals to impact the energy vibrational range of the throat chakra.

Turquoise is a stunningly beautiful stone that can be used when healing the throat chakra. It can be worn and is a common stone used in jewelry. You can also spend time looking at and holding large turquoise stones, and feel the calming energy as it surrounds you and flows through your body.

For truth, use lapis lazuli, a stunning stone with darker blue colors that are not expensive to obtain. You can also use a blue sapphire for this purpose. These stones will help you speak your truth and help you avoid problems related to gossiping or talking badly about others. They will also help you to hold the truth in your dealings with other people and keep your word.

Meditation for the Throat Chakra

The throat chakra is associated with energy levels that are in the blue part of the spectrum, so you will imagine blue lights when you do your basic meditations. Wear blue colors while doing your meditation, and you can fill your meditation space with items that are blue-colored such as pillows, rugs, and drapes. The energy of a room with blue colored carpet can be soft and comforting.

Sit on in the easy pose position. You might want to slightly tilt your head back during this meditation to open up the throat area. I have found it also helps to sit on a blue cushion while doing throat chakra meditations. The addition of a blue cushion helps to bring more blue light energy to the meditation while also helping to elevate the spine a little bit, helping to open the throat chakra.

Close your eyes and begin breathing calmly. See a blue

ball of light against the inky blackness of space, and imagine it slowly approaching you. As the ball of light moves through space, see the shades of blue change, starting from a light shade of baby blue, progressing through turquoise colors, and gradually darkening into the rich blue colors of lapis lazuli stones. Then, see it gradually lighten and have it repeat the color sequence.

See this ball of light come closer and closer, until it is right in front of you, bathing your body in soft blue light. Begin inhaling deeply, and see the light energy enter your lungs, passing through the throat area and healing the larynx. Then see the blue light energy filling your entire body and then exhale, and see the blue light gradually leave the body.

Keep repeating this exercise for 15-30 minutes, with the color of the light changing gradually so that you can inhale the light of different energy levels. This will help you to heal all aspects of the throat chakra, from having insecurity about speaking your own truth to being able to listen to others and heal them.

I have found that when meditating on the spiritual chakras, using guided meditations can be helpful. These can be found in mobile apps or free of charge on YouTube. They can help you with the appropriate colors of light, pleasing music and meditative sounds, and also with mantras. You can spend two to three weeks meditating on the throat chakra, and vary your meditations using multiple methods and techniques.

As we discussed earlier, many aspects of the throat chakra are tied together with the solar plexus and heart chakras. Therefore, you might consider balancing and healing meditation for all three chakras simultaneously.

This is how I do it.

Begin by sitting in the easy pose. Breath calmly and naturally. See a spinning disk of yellow light approaching, and let it enter your body, moving up to the root chakra. Have it moving at a constant speed, slowly moving through the sacral chakra and then coming to rest in the solar plexus. Now, see the size and brightness of the disk of light increase, and visualize bright yellow colors. Feel the pleasing and calming effect of the energy as you watch the disk of light spinning. Have it grow when you breathe in, and shrink a bit when you breathe out. Keep it in the solar plexus chakra for about five minutes, and then see it move out of the solar plexus, gradually moving up toward the heart chakra, and becoming green in color. Have it turn deep and bright green when it reaches the chest area, and let it reside in the heart chakra area for another five minutes, concentrating on the light as you breathe in and out, calmly and methodically. Since the heart chakra is higher energy, have the disk spin faster.

Then see the disk exit the heart chakra area and begin moving up toward the throat chakra. Let it gradually take on blues mixing in with the green color to form shades of turquoise and aquamarine. As it settles into the throat chakra area, feel its warmth bathing and soothing your throat. Let the disk spin faster, taking on higher frequencies of spiritual energy, and let it take on darker shades of blue. You can meditate another five minutes or so on the throat chakra and then see the light gradually fade away to close out your mediation. This mediation will not only help heal all three chakras together, but it will also help to properly balance them.

Affirmations for the Throat Chakra

Although the throat chakra is higher energy, spiritually oriented chakra, it can be strongly influenced by the subconscious mind and the programming that you received throughout your younger years. You can use affirmations to reprogram the throat chakra. The more you say affirmations for the throat chakra, the more they will enter your subconscious mind and reprogram it to initiate better behaviors. The subconscious mind is actually dumb as a computer, and it needs to be told what to do, step-by-step. You have the power to control it using daily affirmations.

- I am able to speak clearly and with confidence.

- I always speak the truth.

- I keep my word, and I am reliable.

- When I am upset about the way I am being treated, I speak out calmly and confidently about it.

- I never get a lump in my throat when I need to speak.

- I am comfortable speaking to others.

- I enjoy public speaking.

- I am a confident speaker.

- The words I speak always contain the truth.

- I enjoy sharing my ideas with others.

- When I communicate through writing, I communicate the truth.

- I am not afraid to voice my opinions.

- I hold myself accountable for speaking the truth.

- I feel safe when speaking my truth to others.

- I will not use communication to hurt other people in any way.

- I speak the truth freely and without fear.

Chapter 8 - Third Eye Chakra

When we get to the third eye chakra, we are entering the realm of purely spiritual chakras. While the throat chakra relates to the connection of the inner world of your mind and ideas to the outer, physical world, the third eye chakra involves connecting to the larger reality that surrounds us. It is through the third eye chakra that we get our intuition and our psychic abilities. Many people have trouble with this because they do not "believe" in the psychic world, but it is not less real than anything else that is experienced; it is a matter of being open to receive it and experience it. When you open your third eye chakra, you will find that you are able to experience other realities than you previously thought possible, and it can help you to become more connected not just to others in your life but also to the spiritual world that exists beyond and is always around us.

What Is the Third Eye Chakra?

The third eye chakra is located in the brow region, in the center just above the physical eyes. Some say that the third eye is actually located in the brain behind this spot, and it is closely associated with the pineal gland. The third eye is an eye, just like the physical eyes. However, it is attuned to other types of energy. It is another way of "seeing" that goes beyond visible light in the physical realm.

The color of the third eye is indigo, which is a bluish-purple color of very high energy. You should not attempt to open the third eye until you feel that your lower chakras are all open and balanced and after gaining some experience with meditation.

The Sanskrit name for the third eye is Ajna. The element of the third eye is light, which reflects its spiritual and high energy nature.

The third eye is timeless, and it transcends physical reality. The third eye can enhance your ways of knowing and help you to see the unseen, learning about the future, as well as the past, and seeing things in the present in ways that cannot be seen using the ordinary physical senses. The third eye represents what people often call the "sixth sense."

Whenever you experience basic intuition, this is a result of the third eye chakra. The third eye chakra can be said to represent gut feelings. You should trust your gut feelings, as these often represent information about people and situations that is important, even if it is "sensed" and not easy to put into words. The spiritual nature of other people is often revealed to us in this manner. That is how it becomes possible to detect whether someone is a good person or not, and we can often use third eye intuition to determine whether or not someone intends to do us harm or not. Sadly, many people reject their intuition because they have been brainwashed by the larger society.

Over the past century, the materialist view of the universe has been ascendant in our culture, gradually becoming more and more accepted. Many people believe that there is no such thing as psychic powers and that intuition is nothing more than an illusion, and your intuitive feelings should be dismissed and not trusted.

This point of view is a mistake, and it discounts the fact that physical reality is not the only reality that there is in this universe. The universe and the living beings that inhabit it have many dimensions to their existence. The higher vibrational frequencies and higher dimensions are of a spiritual nature. They surround and envelop the physical universe. If you are not paying attention, you are not going to be aware of the spiritual aspect of the world. In the past and today, in different cultures, there is a higher level of awareness that allows people to tap into and experience the spiritual realm that they know exists. If you choose to shut it out or discount it, then you are not going to have any awareness of it, and if you experience intuition at all, you will dismiss it as meaningless or as "coincidence."

Since we are trapped in our physical bodies during earthly life, we are not capable of fully experiencing the spiritual world. That is why it is around us only in the form of hints and fleeing experiences. As you become more spiritually developed, the existence of the spiritual world will become clearer and more intense.

Besides intuitive feelings, or experiencing minor events like knowing when a friend is going to call before they do, you can experience information that is revealed to you in dreams. Many people with fully open third eyes experience lucid dreaming. The dreams often reveal events that are going to happen in the future, but you can also have dreams about past life experiences.

The first step to opening up the third eye is to simply allow yourself to have these experiences. Begin by becoming more consciously aware of any psychic or intuitive experiences that you are having. Rather than dismissing them, begin to enhance your awareness. Conscious awareness of spiritual experiences will begin to develop your sense of them. It is just like anything else; when you are not exercising a muscle of a given type, that muscle is going to waste away and not be useful. The same is true when it comes to the third eye, our psychic, and intuitive abilities. They are there, in all of us. But they may be lying dormant if you haven't been exercising them.

The third eye chakra is how you can access your spiritual gifts. Some people tend to think that there are those who are gifted in this realm, while the rest of us lack these abilities. But that is not true. All of us have these abilities; the key is to recognize them, start using them, and increase your awareness of them. There is no limit to the personal power that you can tap by using your psychic abilities.

In order to use the third eye safely, you will need to have your heart and throat chakras open and healed.

The third eye enables us to see hidden truths. It will also provide inner guidance that will help you to get through life's journey more successfully. You will not only be in touch with hidden realities, but you will also come to understand deeper truths and be in touch with realities that cannot be expressed in words or by using logic.

If being mindful is what you seek, opening the third eye can help you get there. Opening the third eye chakra is going to be an essential step for anyone who seeks spiritual growth.

The Unbroken Whole of Reality

Western thought tends to want to breakdown the world into discrete things and steps. You can think of this as the "mechanical" view of the universe that our culture shares. We view the universe and everything in it as being distinct and individualistic.

The true nature of the universe is a duality. The universe does contain discrete individual things and beings within it, but the view that they are independent and completely individualistic is an illusion. At once, while there are individual things and beings, there is also an unbroken whole and totality. You are an individual inside the universe, but you are also the universe itself, a small discrete corner of it that is able to be an isolated individual while also being connected to the unbroken whole.

The third eye is the first chakra that has an aspect that is holistic. The third eye connects you to the fabric of reality beyond. By opening the third eye, you will enhance your ability to see and experience the unbroken totality of all that is. The third eye will help you to connect with your inner wisdom and also the spiritual wisdom that exists as a part of the Higher Self and the Universal Consciousness.

Some people can develop rapidly in their spiritual

growth, and you may find that in addition to lucid dreaming, you are able to experience astral traveling. Do not worry if these abilities do not come to you right away. Everyone will develop their spirituality in unique ways and at their own pace. You may be experiencing astral traveling while in the dream state, and not even be consciously aware of it. Many people dismiss those experiences as "dreams." Try to look at things in a different way and then see how that changes your perceptions of the world.

The third eye chakra can also open up communication with spirit guides. In short, think of the third eye as opening a gateway to the spiritual and the divine. The third eye is the way that you can readily access information and knowledge that comes through means other than the five physical senses.

Wisdom and Ethics

The third eye is also the seat of wisdom. It is through the third eye that you can fully integrate the creativity of the sacral chakra, the self-confidence and leadership characteristics of the solar plexus chakra, and the expressive abilities of the throat chakra. As we have mentioned before, not all ideas are good ideas. But by developing and opening the third eye chakra, you can add a touch of wisdom to the creative forces that originate in the sacral chakra, and turn your ideas toward the good of humanity and of all life.

Opening the third eye will also help you become more balanced, tolerant, and open-minded. A strong connection to your own inner wisdom, as well as the collective wisdom of the Universal Consciousness, is a benefit of a third eye awakening.

There are different aspects of psychic awareness that

different people will tune into to different degrees. Lucid dreaming may be stronger in some people as compared to others. Some will become clairvoyant, which means you are "clear seeing," and able to receive visions. These visions may be visions of the future, or they may provide knowledge of information and events that you could not be aware of through normal means. Others will develop a strong sense of clairaudience, which means "clear hearing," where information is revealed in the form of sounds or voices. **Claircognizance** is simply clear-knowing, which means you will suddenly "know" something.

All of us have these gifts to one degree or another, so they are not mutually exclusive. Don't worry about having one or the other or getting bogged down in focusing on the individual definitions. Instead, let yourself experience things as they come to you. Simply being open will reveal the experiences to you in due time.

The third eye is also closely associated with your direction in life and your sense of purpose. Often, this is going to be experienced as a higher sense of purpose. It will be a sense of purpose that transcends mere career or material aspirations. It may also take the form of a sense of purpose that goes beyond individualism and is communal, spiritual, and ethical in nature.

How the Third Eye Chakra Gets Blocked?

The third eye can become blocked when your experiences are discounted. For example, many of us have spiritual or psychic experiences but are mocked when we share them with others. When you are younger, especially in childhood, having your experiences

94

discounted or mocked can have a large impact on the third eye, causing it to become blocked.

Our larger society also causes many people to have a blocked third eye. The larger society has adopted a viewpoint that is materialistic in outlook. The larger society believes there is nothing beyond the physical world and that science is all that there is and the only way of knowing. It discounts psychic experiences and writes off intuition as wishful thinking or coincidence. Belief in spirituality is seen as quaint, and spiritual experiences are deemed to be illusions, the product of an overactive mind, or even the product of mental illness.

We are not consciously aware of it, but when these attitudes are all around us, constantly expressed and pervasive, they infuse and train the subconscious, making it more difficult for us to open the third eye and to doubt any psychic or intuitive experiences that we have. Without realizing it, we may even adopt a skeptical attitude steeped in materialism and scientism that prevents us from experiencing the full richness of the world that is around us.

The third eye can also become blocked as a result of traumatic experiences. Any experience that leaves you with post-traumatic stress disorder or lingering effects of abuse that occurred during childhood can work to block the third eye.

Symptoms of a Third Eye Chakra Blockage

We all have an inner voice, and the first symptom of a third eye blockage is that you discount or ignore the inner voice. Many people can even get in a position where the inner voice is silenced. When this happens,

95

they will become dull to the information that is being revealed to them through the sixth sense.

Fear of the future is one symptom of a third eye blockage. This happens because the tapestry of time is a continuous flow, with the past connected to the present, which is connected to future. This connection is of a psychic nature, and when you cut it off, you may find yourself feeling an overwhelming sense of uncertainty that can lead to a fear of the future. Anxiety can often come about as a result.

If you are experiencing anxiety, you might want to take a close look at it so that you can determine the origins of this anxiety. Remember that when your root chakra becomes blocked, anxiety can develop. To distinguish that type of anxiety from the anxiety that can arise from a third eye blockage, take a look at what the anxiety is focused on. When you feel anxiety about your basic safety and security, this means that the anxiety is more closely related to the root chakra. When the anxiety is mainly future-directed, it can be the result of a third eye blockage. Often, the blockages of both chakras can occur at the same time, as it is impossible to have truly healthy higher chakras when your root chakra is blocked. If you are experiencing anxiety, it is a good idea to work on root chakra meditations and then do some meditating on the third eye chakra.

Excessive skepticism is one of the main symptoms of a third eye blockage. When people have a third eye blockage, they actually try to "rationalize" it by focusing on logic and overwhelming skepticism. You have probably met people who are skeptical of everything, always demanding to see proof of any event or phenomenon. These people are excessively steeped in the scientific way of thinking. Science is a valid tool, and it has many uses in our society, but the problem results when science takes on a role that is more akin to religious thought, rather than viewing it as the tool that it is. Unfortunately, viewing science in religious terms is becoming more widespread in our society. This is leading to more and more people having their third eye and crown chakras blocked, as the attitude of scientism is beginning to become pervasive and integrated with our lifestyle, which has become focused on materialistic consumerism.

This brings us to another point that illustrates the symptoms of a blocked third eye chakra. And that is, when the third eye is blocked, some people become obsessively materialistic. When the third eye is blocked, you are actually blocking off an important aspect of your identity. A human being is far more than just a physical being. Rather, a human being is a whole and a complete entity that is made up of the physical being, the mental and emotional being, and the spiritual being. When the third eye and crown chakra are blocked, we are cutting off the spiritual essence that makes us whole and complete.

This creates a void that will exist in our lives. This void has to be filled in some way, so people try filling it through meaningless materialism. One way this occurs is that they fill their life with material goods, thinking that buying fancy clothing, jewelry, and electronic gadgets is going to fill their inner needs and make their lives whole. Another way that they try to fill the void is through the pursuit of endless entertainment. Our society is more than willing and able to provide mindless entertainment, through endless arrays of tv programs, sporting events, video games, and pornography. Of course, it is good and healthy to relax with one or more of these things as a part of a balanced life. But many people are attempting to fill every minute of their existence with some form of entertainment because they have a blocked third eye chakra, and they are completely cut off from the spiritual and psychic aspects of their existence.

One problem with this is that these attempts to replace the spiritual with the material and entertainment never work. This leaves people feeling as though their lives are meaningless, and it can lead to an existential crisis in some people. They may attempt to fill the void with drugs and alcohol, and you can end up with a blocked sacral chakra in addition to the blocked third eye.

So, we can summarize the symptoms of a blocked third eye chakra as including heightened or excessive skepticism, a feeling, and belief that the material world is all that exists, that life has no meaning, and there is also a vague but pervasive sense that your own life is without purpose. You might have a career and a healthy solar plexus chakra, but if your third eye is blocked, you will have trouble having a sense of purpose and meaning that is associated with your life and work. Depression is a common symptom of a blocked third eye chakra, and as we discussed, anxiety about the future can also indicate that the third eye chakra is blocked or in need of healing.

The third eye can also become overactive. Once again, we can think of what the third eye chakra is associated with when it is functioning in a normal and healthy manner, and how this can be turned around when the third eye is overactive. The first thing that can happen is that psychic information becomes excessive and intrusive. This can lead to the experience of delusions, as information flood gates may become open, filling your mind with information that is not necessarily relevant to you or even real. When the third eye is overactive, you might have auditory and visual hallucinations. This is because too much information is going to be flooding in, to the point that it might start overwhelming your senses, and you might start occupying a place of meaninglessness that is straddling the psychic and physical worlds.

The overactive information that is impacting your senses might impact your mind as well. When this happens, paranoid thinking patterns can result. This is a phenomenon that occurs when intuitive information is open to the point of being a flood, and it is picked up by the mind, rather than by the physical senses. Often, this information is misinterpreted because a person having these experiences is not necessarily aware of the third eye and genuine intuition.

Another symptom of a third eye blockage is that the mind is excessively ego-based. This is because when the third eye is open, you become in touch with the universe beyond and the Universal Consciousness, and the ego begins to play a diminished role in your perceptions. In contrast, when the third eye is blocked, this puts you in a situation where excessive amounts of energy can be concentrated in the root, sacral, and solar plexus chakras. That, in turn, leads to a higher level of focus on the self and your own needs. It also diminishes the connection that you have with the rest of the universe.

When the third eye is blocked, you are not able to see the totality of reality accurately. This can leave people feeling cynical and disconnected, and put them in a position where they have a tendency to blame others or external circumstances for their position in their life. When the third eye is blocked, you are cutting yourself off from a great deal of wisdom and spiritual connection that goes beyond the self.

The ability to visualize becomes limited when the third eye is blocked. The third eye is not just involved with psychic phenomena. In fact, it is also involved in the type of visualization that leads to the invention of new things, great artwork, or the imagination required to write a play, develop a movie, or start a new business. An open third eye will help your imagination soar and open up many new possibilities. In contrast, when the third eye is blocked, you will become unimaginative and trapped in the here and now. Many of the great figures of society, from Da Vinci to Mozart to Steve Jobs, were calling on the power of the third eye to spark their imaginations. People who are very creative not only have an open sacral chakra, but they also have an open third eye as well. Many creative insights come from a connection with the Universal Consciousness. In fact, when you speak to many creative people, they will report that they don't really know where their insights come from; they often seem to just "appear."

A blocked third eye can limit your creative abilities by shutting off this connection. People who are just getting by in life, working only to meet their needs for survival and perhaps hoping to reach retirement and be comfortable, are often people with a blocked third eye chakra.

When the third eye is blocked, your ability to visualize when trying to see something in the future is one of the capacities of the human spirit that becomes limited or eliminated altogether. This is why the world's leading creative people are literally able to change the world. Through the third eye, they are able to not only see the world as it is, but they can see the world as an array of multiple possibilities in the future. Thomas Edison is an example of a historical figure, who, consciously or not, was able to utilize the third eye to help him see things that did not yet exist and imagine how they would transform society and enable people to live in new and different ways.

People with a blocked third eye will also suffer from indecisiveness. This is going to have its largest impact when they are required to make choices about their future course in life. Indecision can plague them, leading them to a place where they often fail to take action, or they never feel satisfied by the choices that they do manage to make.

Believe it or not, a lack of common sense is also a sign of a blocked third eye chakra. We are seeing this expressed in the larger culture of late, where the attainment of an 'education' is being elevated, and everyday common sense is being denigrated. Don't misunderstand; we are not knocking out the idea of getting more education, but don't elevate it at the expense of common sense and intuition, which are two of your most important gifts.

Nightmares

This symptom deserves special mention. If your third eye becomes blocked or overactive, you might find that you suffer from extremely vivid and unpleasant dreams or nightmares. Often, these dreams will entail a spiritual component that feels like an evil presence. You may wake up from these dreams feeling threatened and uncomfortable. If these types of dreams become recurrent, this is a definite symptom that you are having problems related to the third eye chakra. Immediate attention should be devoted to meditation, affirmations, and the use of crystals to help direct the correct energy.

The Pineal Gland

The third eye is said, by some, to originate from the pineal gland, a small organ that is closely associated with the brain. Many in the medical community will assert that the pineal gland serves no useful purpose, but in fact, it is a relay station of sorts when it comes to the reception and transmission of psychic energy. The pineal gland can become calcified, and one of the most important factors in the calcification of this important organ is the consumption of fluoridated water. If you can eliminate the use of water with fluoride in it from your body, then you will go a long way toward healing and decalcifying the pineal gland. By itself, for some people, this is enough to open and awaken their third eye. There are many supplements and tonics you can take to detoxify and decalcify the pineal gland.

The pineal gland is closely associated with our sleep-wake cycle, and when the pineal gland is calcified, you may find that your sleep-wake cycle is impaired. Your circadian rhythm may not be properly tuned to the daylight cycle our bodies are naturally designed for, and you might find that you are a so-called "night owl." You might have trouble getting a full night's sleep and have to take naps often.

Excessive calcium intake can lead to calcification of the pineal gland. To get appropriate levels of calcium, avoid supplements, and get calcium from natural sources instead. There are many natural sources of calcium that can help you get adequate levels, including whole milk, cheese, and leafy green vegetables, like spinach. Avoid synthetic calcium, if possible.

Many people worry about fluoridated toothpaste, but in truth, it is fluoride in the water that is the main concern. If you can eliminate the consumption of fluoridated water, then toothpaste should not be an issue. Just avoid swallowing toothpaste, and the amount of fluoride you will be exposed to, in that case, will be minimal and inconsequential.

In order to decalcify the pineal gland, there are many supplements you can take. The primary substance that people turn to, for this purpose, is iodine. You can take iodine supplements or drops for this purpose. You can also increase the amount of iodine that you are consuming by eating sea kelp. Consider adding dried seaweed to soups, broths, and meals.

Turmeric is also believed to help decalcify the pineal gland by inhibiting the toxic effects of getting too much fluoride in the body. If you continue to use fluoridated toothpaste, a turmeric supplement can help keep you healthy and in balance.

A supplement known as Activator X is also considered helpful when it comes to the pineal gland. Activator X contains the vitamins K1 and K2, which are important for overall health, in addition to assisting with the pineal gland.

Physical Symptoms of a Blocked Third Eye Chakra

A blockage of the third eye chakra can manifest with physical symptoms. Pay special attention to these symptoms if they are accompanied by any of the mental and emotional symptoms of a blocked third eye chakra.

Chronic headaches, including migraines, can indicate that there is a third eye chakra. Insomnia is also an important symptom of third eye blockages, especially when it is accompanied by vivid nightmares.

Eye pain or pain in the front of the skull or in the temple region can be the result of a third eye blockage. You might also have visual disturbances or a rapid decline in visual quality. Many people who wear contact lenses will report that their contact lenses no longer seem to work. Your eyes might also feel dry, painful, and irritated. Scratchy feelings may also develop when there is a blockage of the third eye chakra.

Third Eye Awakening

If you start meditating on the third eye, do not be alarmed if you notice unusual symptoms. You might start to feel a pressure sensation in the center of your brow. This is entirely natural, as there is energy flowing through the third eye as it begins to open. You might also experience ringing of the ears, and other unusual symptoms as the third eye fully opens, maybe for the very first time in your life since childhood. You might also be awakened by vivid dreams. Do not be alarmed by this unless the dreams that you are experiencing are of a negative character. Again, as mentioned before, if you have dreams that are negative and extremely vivid or heavy nightmares, then use third eye meditation to rectify the problem. When your third eye is awakened, you are going to have lucid dreaming, but the dreams are not going to be frightening in any way. Rather, the dreams will serve to inform, convey, and enlighten. The dreams that you have when the third eye has been awakened may be so vivid that they are indistinguishable from reality. This is because, in a sense, they are real. Prepare yourself for his possibility by meditation and other techniques.

By healing the heart and throat chakras, you can help to ensure that your experience of a third eye awakening will be positive in nature. Often, the experiences that we have while moving into the more spiritual aspects of the chakras are going to depend on the overall level of spiritual development and growth that you have had up to this point. If you are unprepared, you might find that you are unleashing energies that you are ill-equipped to deal with. That can lead to nightmares, bad visions, and other problems. So one thing to consider if you find yourself having negative experiences, such as bad dreams, is to take a step back and work on the heart chakra first. Then work on the throat chakra.

Think about the impact of opening up spiritual and psychic energies when you are steeped in negativity, and possibly lacking love, acceptance, empathy, and truth. This is why it is important to work on the lower chakras before attempting a third eye awakening. All of the chakras should be involved in this process. For example, you need to have a healthy root chakra so that you have an overall sense of safety and security. You also need to have a healthy solar plexus chakra because that chakra is involved in self-confidence and self-assurance, and both of these are going to be important for the ability to accept and manage powerful, intuitive, and psychic energies.

It is also important to recognize that evil does exist in the world and in the universe. That is one reason that awakening the third eye without a basic grounding can lead to problems. Don't misinterpret this. We are not saying that you are a bad person, only that these energies are out there, and they can be stirred up when a person is not properly prepared.

This is why working on the heart chakra is so important. Evil energies can be nullified with love and understanding. By fully healing and opening up the heart chakra, you can maximize the love energy in your spirit. Doing so to the point of attaining higher levels of development is necessary. You will be able to recognize when you have reached this point when you feel and experience unconditional love, empathy, and forgiveness for all humankind.

From here, it is important to ensure that the throat chakra is fully open and healed. Remember our discussion of the throat chakra and how we discussed the impact of gossip or speaking for untrue or bad purposes and the importance of keeping your word. These may sound like basic values, but in fact, they also go straight to the heart of spiritual coherence. The foundation of the good begins with truth. In fact, you can say that truth is central to the concept of good, as opposed to the concept of evil, which finds a friend in deception and lies. From this perspective, you can start to appreciate how important it is to heal the throat chakra, in addition to healing the heart chakra, before you attempt a third eye awakening and connect yourself at a spiritual level to worlds beyond our physical universe.

Foods for the Third Eye Chakra

When you are working on healing and opening the third eye chakra, think in terms of dark-colored and purple foods. Grapes (red, purple, and black), blackberry, and blueberries are excellent foods to include in your diet when you are working on the third eye. In addition, consume eggplant, purple carrots, and purple potatoes.

The idea of mindful eating is also important for the third eye chakra. Remember that with the third eye chakra, we have completely entered the realm of the spiritual. Therefore, your intention and purpose while eating can have an influence on the opening of your third eye. Also, use your intuition. Sometimes, the third eye makes itself known through small signs, and we might not really be aware of them. You can heighten your intuitive abilities by paying more attention to the slightest intuitive impulse.

Intuition often makes itself felt when you are making food choices. When you notice that your intuition strikes when it comes to a food choice, rather than overthinking it or worse, doubting the intuition, follow it instead, and consume the foods that your third eye is directing you to consume.

Other foods that help with the third eye are those that are rich in omega-three fatty acids. Try bluefish, salmon, and mackerel. Walnuts are also good for the third eye, and the role that omega-three fatty acids play in protecting brain health is a more practical way that the third eye and the pineal gland can be enhanced.

Essential Oils for the Third Eye Chakra

Aromatherapy and essential oils play a more important role for the third eye and crown chakras than for the lower chakras. Look for powerful holy oils like frankincense and myrrh. Clary, which is made from a purple flower, is also useful for the third eye chakra. Juniper is also helpful. Use aromatherapy to help awaken the third eye and for balance.

Colors for the Third Eye Chakra

The third eye chakra is associated with indigo, which is a bluish-purple color. You can use dark blue colors, along with purple colors when healing the third eye. Due to the spiritual nature of this chakra, I like to involve the use of candles when working on opening it. Use purple or, if you can find them, blue colored candles together. You can light the candles at any time and breathe in the aromas to help unlock third eye energy. It can also be helpful to use purple candles during meditation sessions. You can also decorate your meditation space with dark blue and purple colored items, and wear purple clothing.

Crystals for the Third Eye Chakra

Purple amethyst is a favorite crystal when it comes to the third eye chakra. Typically, this crystal will manifest multiple colors, including white and sometimes, bits of gold. This is a powerful crystal that can channel spiritual level energies. Use it while meditating or as a touchstone, when you are interested in unblocking the third eye. You can also use lapis lazuli with the third eye. This dark blue stone is able to channel energies for the third eye and for the throat chakra, and it is more attuned to the higher vibrational states of the throat chakra and is, therefore, more spiritual in nature. It can be helpful to use it because keeping the throat chakra open and healed is an important part of a third eye awakening.

Meditation for the Third Eye Chakra

When meditating for the third eye, try and focus the energy toward the midpoint of the brow. As always, you can meditate in the easy pose, with eyes closed, and you can use regular breathing. When you begin your meditation, focus your attention on the location of the third eye. As you breathe, become consciously aware of the sensations of pressure, heat, and energy that you may get in the center of the brow region. As you do this, imagine a ball of purple light coming toward you. See it in the dark but extremely fluorescent and vibrant purple colors. Allow the light to come toward you and see it emit a beam of energy. Let the beam of energy connect to the center of your brow at the location of the third eye chakra. Now, see it go all the way through your head, and have it exit at the back of the head. The third eye is often viewed as extending all the way through the brain toward the back of the head, so it is the reason it is useful to see the beam of light go all the way through. Meditate on this for 15 minutes, and then see the beam of light shut off, and the energy ball gradually disappear before your eyes. You may be feeling exhausted by this experience and breathing heavily, so focus on your breath and return to a state of calmness as you end your meditation session.

Some people find that they are able to enhance the energy flow into the third eye by holding their hands in the prayer position during their meditation sessions. You can also try this any time during the day when you need "mini" healing or meditation. Simply close your eyes and put your hands in the prayer position, and then allow the energy to pass through the brow region, concentrating on that area and becoming fully aware of all the sensations that you are experiencing.

Affirmations for the Third Eye Chakra

In this section, we will review some affirmations that are useful for the third eye chakra.

- I am trusting and worthy of receiving intuitive knowledge.

- I trust my intuition.

- I will listen to my inner voice.

- I am open to imagination and visualization.

- I will receive knowledge that the universe has to give.

- I trust my feelings and will listen to them.

- I seek inner wisdom and guidance.

- I trust in the light of the Universal Consciousness.

- I am open and accepting.

- I am intuitive.

- I accept Higher Truths.

- I let my sixth sense guide me to the truth.

- Spiritual truth is the realm of unlimited possibilities.

The crown chakra is the highest and most spiritual of all the chakras. In this chapter, we will examine the crown chakra and explore the role it plays in your life and how you can open and heal the crown chakra. Before healing the crown chakra or attempting to reach this level of spirituality, you should ensure that the other chakras are healed and in balance. This means you must heal the root, sacral, solar plexus, heart, throat, and third eye chakras before attempting to open the crown chakra.

Opening the crown chakra is going to be an important

part of your spiritual growth. Patience is key. Do not attempt to open the crown chakra until you have successfully opened the other chakras and gone through the process of spiritual growth that accompanies going through each of the chakras one by one.

After you open the crown chakra, you can elevate your spirituality, pursuing a full third eye awakening, and a kundalini awakening. Again, be patient and grow in time. Following the natural order of things, this spiritual opening will happen according to the way that it should happen.

What Is the Crown Chakra?

The crown chakra represents the highest level of our spirituality and the connection between our spiritual self and the Universal Consciousness. In addition to connecting to the universal consciousness, the crown chakra represents our connection to our own Higher Self. So the crown chakra can be taken to represent the connection between our physical and mental bodies, and the spiritual body or Higher Self. At the same time, it is connected to the ultimate duality of the universe that we inhabit, in that we are able to connect our individuality to the Universal Consciousness beyond.

The crown chakra is taken to exist at the top or crown of the head, although some observers say that the crown chakra actually exists at a physical location slightly outside the body and above the crown of the head. The exact location is not going to be important for your studies or spiritual growth or your meditations.

The colors of the crown chakra are a multitude, as it has great spiritual significance. The crown chakra has purple as its main color, reflecting the higher vibrational state of this most energetic of the chakras. Remember that purple is the highest possible energy state that visible light can assume. As such, since this is the highest energy state of the chakras, purple is associated with it.

The crown chakra is also associated with the color white, as well. This is because the crown chakra, in some sense, represents the unity of all the other chakras. And what is the color white? It is a mixture of all the colors of the rainbow. As such, the crown chakra assumes the color white to represent the root, sacral, solar plexus, heart, throat, third eye, and crown chakras all mixed together and in balance. The more abundant the white light is in your life, the more balanced you are.

The crown chakra also embodies the color of gold. The mixture or blending of the colors purple, white, and gold is the color of royalty and of godliness. As we will see, these colors can be combined together and represented in a single crystal.

In Sanskrit, the crown chakra is called **Sahasrara**. It is also referred to as Niralambapuri and Shunnya. Think of the crown chakra as a thousand-petaled purple lotus flower. There is no element associated with the crown chakra because it is considered to represent the connection with the divine, so it cannot be associated with any physical element. If it can be associated with a physical element, we will note that the third eye chakra is associated with light itself. Therefore, the crown chakra could be associated with an entity like the Higgs Boson field that fills the entire universe and gives everything and anything energy and meaning.

Tapping into the power of the crown chakra is going to be the pinnacle of your spiritual growth before you reach more advanced states of being like a kundalini awakening.

The crown chakra can be associated with the pituitary gland, and this is the way that our physical bodies are connected with the reality that exists beyond our imaginations.

Energetically, imagine your body forming a loop. The energy can connect from the top of the head down to the base of the spine, forming a loop between the crown chakra and the root chakra, through which energy flows as you open each of the chakras in your meditations.

In its relation to the physical body, the crown chakra is closely associated with the brain and the nervous system. But it goes well beyond the physical realm. The crown chakra connects your mind, body, and soul to the spiritual realms of existence.

People often want to know and understand how they can connect each of the chakras to their daily existence. The crown chakra is no exception. Fortunately, the crown chakra is well-understood by yogi practitioners and gurus, and everyone can unlock their crown chakra and harness its power.

The crown chakra, first and foremost, is connected to the brain itself and to consciousness. The brain, by itself, would be nothing more than a meaningless pile of matter, a ball of mush. It is through the connection to the crown chakra and the spiritual reality that lies beyond that the brain becomes animated. It is through this ongoing and dynamic process that consciousness arises.

But mere consciousness is only the tip of the iceberg when it comes to the crown chakra. In fact, the crown chakra is what helps to connect our physical existence to higher spirituality in deep ways. The third eye chakra does this as well to a certain extent, but it is through the crown chakra that we are able to connect to the sacred.

Remember that the universe is a universe that has a dual nature. That is, the universe has a nature that is connected through the physical, where there is an individuality of beings and things. Yet, at the same time, the universe is one single unbroken whole. The crown chakra is the linkage point between these two dual natures of existence. It is through the crown chakra that we, as individuals, can connect to the formless and timeless nature of all that is. That is, we can link up with the Universal Consciousness that is at once surrounding us and at the same time, a vital part of our own conscious being.

Through our crown chakra, we can also connect with spirit guides and the past spirits that have had a role to play in our lives. Through the crown chakra, you are able to reunite with past loved ones, including family members, friends, and beings that we considered to be "pets" in our conscious existence. We can also connect with Spirit Guides that can connect us to the infinite wisdom that lies beyond the physical world. As such, through the crown chakra, you are able to achieve a communion with higher states of being that simply is not possible otherwise.

People who have opened the crown chakra will feel a deep connection to and a love for all living beings. This is a state of pure bliss that exists without judgment or any other characteristic that we can experience in the ordinary physical world, which is based on ego and competition. There is an unbroken whole that represents the Divine, and we are a part of it. With the duality of the Universe at hand, we know that as individuals who exist as a part of this Divine whole, and yet we are the Divine itself, we must go through a learning phase where we grow to the point where we can become a part of it, and achieve a trust state of bliss, unity, and harmony.

Opening the crown chakra will provide a gateway to your Higher Self and allow you to attain a state of peace, harmony, and bliss.

How the Crown Chakra Gets Blocked?

Many things can serve to block the crown chakra, including blockages of lower charkas. In fact, this will surprise many due to its lower location, but a blockage of the heart chakra can cause a blockage of your crown chakra. The reason is that the heart chakra is closely associated with our connection to other people and living beings. Although the heart chakra is associated with our connection to physical beings in the here and now, any connection to a conscious, living entity is associated with a spiritual connection. If you are unable to make a basic connection between yourself and other living, physical beings, this is going to inhibit your ability to form connections with the spiritual world that exists beyond.

As a result, shallow and disconnected or dysfunctional relationships in your physical world can cause your crown chakra to become blocked.

An overdeveloped or hyperactive ego can also lead to a blockage of the crown chakra. While we emphasize the development of a healthy solar plexus chakra, when considering the building and development of the lower, matter-based chakras, we can actually block the crown chakra if we overemphasize the solar plexus chakra and it becomes unbalanced. This is because the solar plexus chakra is associated with the development and elevation of the self or ego, which causes a hyper-development of the self if this is carried too far. In contrast, the crown chakra emphasizes the communion of the self with the Universal Consciousness. It is important to realize that this communion of the self with the Universal Consciousness does not involve the obliteration of the self. Rather, it involves the joining of the self with the larger, and pervasive, universal consciousness. That is, although it may be difficult for you to understand now, it involves the retainment of the self while simultaneously joining your consciousness, together with the unified whole that represents the universe.

Symptoms of a Crown Chakra Blockage

Like the third eye, a blocked crown chakra can manifest in the form of a cynical attitude that dismisses spirituality or the belief in a nonphysical aspect of existence. Also, since the crown chakra is closely associated with connectivity, both with living, conscious beings, as well as with the Universal Consciousness beyond, a feeling of being disconnected from others is an important symptom of a crown chakra that is blocked.

As we saw with the third eye chakra, since the crown chakra is a purely spiritual chakra, closed-mindedness and skepticism are attitudes that are often invoked when one has a blocked crown chakra. Someone who always demands physical proof for things is someone who is experiencing a blockage of the crown chakra.

Some people actually have an overactive crown chakra. As a result, they may feel disconnected from their bodies. When learning about the chakras and your relationship with them, it is important to keep the duality of man in mind throughout the process. This means that balance is always the key to a healthy crown chakra or any of the other chakras. If you are still living in the physical body, there is a reason for this. You must learn the lessons of the physical body in order to evolve spiritually. As such, it can become a big mistake to go so beyond the physical body, that while you are to live in the physical body, you become detached from it.

When you have a blocked crown chakra, you are going to be someone who is a disbeliever in any kind of existence beyond the physical world. Like those with a blocked third eye, you are going to be an overactive skeptic, prone to scientism, and not believing that there is any kind of existence beyond the here and now.

Many people with blocked crown chakras doubt the existence of a conscious mind, and they doubt that other living beings like "animals" have any kind of experience of self-consciousness or life that could possibly exist beyond the physical body.

When you have a blocked crown chakra, one thing that is going to be missing from your life is a sense of purpose. As we have seen throughout the book, a missing sense of purpose is something that can manifest across many different chakras. However, one thing that distinguishes the crown chakra is that if you feel that your life lacks any kind of purpose, you are going to have an **existential** sense about this if a crown chakra blockage is involved.

Even though the crown chakra is spiritual in nature, if you have a blocked crown chakra, this is going to impact your ability to connect with others. This can lead to feelings of isolation and loneliness. You can also feel disconnected from family members, despite the obvious bloodlines. You may also feel disconnected spiritually and even angry. Many people will feel disconnected spiritually when they have a blocked crown chakra, but they will proclaim themselves to be atheists or nonbelievers. Some will profess anger against God, blaming God for their lot in life and failure to attain levels of success that they believe are their birthright.

Another symptom of a blocked crown chakra that might not seem obvious at first is an inability to set and reach goals. This is a difficult problem to crack because other chakra blockages can cause similar symptoms. In particular, we know that a blocked solar plexus chakra can make it difficult for you to carry out your plans. As a result, it is often hard to distinguish between a blockage of that type and one that is higher up in energy, impacting the crown chakra. One clue is that in the case of the solar plexus chakra, the goals that you want to reach tend to be more physical, ego-based, and simple. When you have a blocked crown chakra, you might find that you are unable to meet lofty or spiritual goals. If you are unsure, working on all the chakras is something that can always lead you to the right path.

Nonetheless, a lack of direction in a general sense is something that is always tied to a blockage of the crown chakra. This is because a healthy and open crown chakra is something that is going to be closely associated with someone who is able to set and achieve goals, and who knows exactly where they are going.

An overactive crown chakra can also manifest in the form of an excessive attachment to the spiritual side of existence. It is true that we are spiritual beings. And it is also true that at some point, we will experience our entire existence through a spiritual body. But at the present time, you are, in part, a physical body, and you are going through the lessons in the physical universe because you need to go through those lessons. Attempting to get through life by becoming obsessively attached to the spiritual is not a sign of spiritual growth. Instead, it is a sign that you are failing to grow and develop in a way that you should. If you are here on planet earth, it is because you need to learn the lessons of physical life. An obsessive existence based on spiritual concerns only is actually an indication that you are not spiritually growing and developing in a proper manner. Or, put another way, it is a sign that your crown chakra is not properly balanced.

The physical symptoms of the crown chakra blockage tend to be related to the nervous system. The most common physical symptom of blockage is migraine headaches. You might also experience blurred vision. Other symptoms include dizziness, blackouts, and seizures. In extreme cases, particularly when the blockage has lasted for an extremely long time period, it can manifest in the form of neurological diseases, like ALS, Parkinson's disease, and Alzheimer's. Blindness, hearing loss, and stroke can also happen.

Foods for the Crown Chakra

When thinking of foods for the crown chakra, think broadly. White-colored foods like white or yellow carrots and white cauliflower are additions to your diet that can definitely help heal the crown chakra. Moreover, you can include purple foods like eggplant, blueberries, and purple potatoes that we have discussed in conjunction with other chakras. For the crown chakra, it is beneficial to make meals that consist of a mixture of the colors purple, white, and gold, into a single meal. With this in mind, consider mixing together blueberries or blackberries for purple, white potatoes or cauliflower for white, and corn and butter for gold, in order to build a complete meal for unblocking the crown chakra. Other yellow or golden foods can be helpful for the crown chakra, including yellow squash, carrots, parsnip, almond, walnut, and sesame seeds.

Essential Oils for the Crown Chakra

When it comes to essential oils for the crown chakra, the spiritual or holy oils are the best oils to use. Frankincense is an excellent oil to include when healing the crown chakra. It will help you to attain a state of meditative contemplation, spiritual connection, and openness. Vetiver is a good essential oil to use with aromatherapy or in conjunction with other essential oils to promote the healing of the crown chakra. Moreover, this oil can be used to work with the third eye because it promotes vivid dreaming. It will also help you to recall your dreams, which is an important way to promote spiritual awareness. This oil also promotes grounding and relaxation, so it can help you to open your crown chakra. To elevate the frequency of vibration, consider adding helichrysum. This less well-known essential oil is also known as everlasting oil. This essential oil contains energies that are of a higher frequency of vibration and, hence, more spiritual in nature. This high frequency of vibration can help you to unleash the power of your crown chakra.

Colors for the Crown Chakra

The main color for the crown chakra is a deep purple. Pure white, representing the mixture of all the colors of the rainbow, is also an important color associated with the crown chakra. Gold is also associated with the crown chakra, due to its elevation as a spiritual concept. You can wear all of them together when you are working to heal the crown chakra.

Crystals for the Crown Chakra

There are several crystals that are useful for healing and opening the crown chakra. Purple amethyst, which is also used with the third eye chakra, can be of great assistance when healing the crown chakra. This stone vibrates with high frequency, and it can store, receive, and transmit large amounts of energy. White-colored stones are also useful, including clear quartz and plain quartz. If you have access to it, pure gold is also helpful for work with the crown chakra.

Meditation for the Crown Chakra

For meditation with the crown chakra, I like to do a complete balancing mediation. Use the standard mediation procedure, but have a disk of light go through each of the major chakras, moving up through your body and spinning faster as it gains energy. As it passes through each of the seven major chakras, have it change color as appropriate, moving through red, orange, yellow, green, blue, indigo, and purple. When it exits your body at the top of the head, see it as a white light beaming upward toward heaven, connecting you to the Universal Consciousness.

Affirmations for the Sacral Chakra

- I am complete.

- I am a spiritual being.

- The universe is kind and loving.

- I am connected to the universe and to all that is.

- I am connected to my Spirit Guides.

- I am a light being.

- I am perfect as is, and I accept myself as is.
- I am loved, and the universe is pure love.

CPSIA information can be obtained
at www.ICGtesting.com
Printed in the USA
LVHW082305200821
695738LV00002B/130